DISCLAIMER AND LEGAL STUFF

In offering this work to the reader, the author c... reader will achieve the level of training he has achieved wit... he success of training a dog including breed, age, knowledg... nation and dedication. This book simply outlines the factors... a hunter / writer who has enjoyed a long, successful and re... ......u with his current lurcher (arguably one of the most written about and photographed hunting dogs in the UK over recent years). The author wishes you equal success with training your own pup but in no way underwrites that buying this book will guarantee it.

Any reference to hunting, animal welfare and national law in this book are based on current UK legislation. The author will not be held responsible for any misinterpretation of the content

All text, photographs and illustrations in this work were created and supplied by the author and remain his copyright.

© Ian Barnett 2014

DEDICATION

Who else could I dedicate this book to but Dylan the Lurcher, my faithful hunting hound.
As I write, nearly eleven years by my side in triumph and in defeat. Some we missed, but most, we got! Through rain and snow and mud and drought. One day shivering, another parched.
Never perfect but .. usually .. proficient, just like his Master. At times, temperamental and moody .. just like his Master. Right more times than he was wrong in his hunting decisions .. unlike his Master. Feral and determined in the field but unbelievably soft in domesticity. Yep! Just like his Master!

Contents

Dedication ....

Foreword ....

Of Man and Dog ....

What Type Of Dog? ....

Good Dog, Bad Dog? ....

                         General Good Manners ....

                         Barking ....

                         Jumping Up ....

                         Toilet Manners ....

                         Begging ....

                         Aggression ....

                         Socialisation ....

                         Car Etiquette ....

Body Language ....

                         The Tail That Wags The Dog ....

                         The Tale Of Two Dogs ....

                         The Eyes Have It ....

                         Bad Health Signals ....

                         Dogs And The Weather ....

                         Alien Encounters ....

Homing, Feeding and Exercise ....

A Pup Settles In ....

Some Basic Training Rules ....

        Alpha / Beta Principles ....

        The One-Dog Principle ....

        Think Like A Dog ....

The Training 'Commands' ....

        'Sit' ....

        'Get On' or 'Go On'! ....

        'Get here' or 'come back' ....

        Lead Training ....

        'Heel' or 'Wait' ....

        'Drop' ....

        'Go Fetch!' ....

        'Stay' ....

        'Leave!' ....

        'Over 'and 'Jump' ....

The bridge encounter ....

        'Look about' ....

        'Catch!' ....

Introducing The Pup To Hunting ....

        Your Dogs Vocabulary ....

Silent Commands ....

Health & Welfare..

Permission and Stitches ....

An Unexpected Rabbit..

The Later Years..

The Paparazzi Pooch..

The Last Word – From Dylan ....

Postscript...

About The Author..

Foreword

I am not an out-and-out dog trainer. Nor have I ever set out to train my hunting hounds to comply with the competition-type discipline demanded by field-trialling devotees. I am a hunter. My preferred shooting discipline, upon which I have built a solid reputation in the UK as a photo-journalist and author, is small vermin hunting with the air rifle. Throughout hundreds of magazine articles, blogs and two published books on the subject there has been a stalwart companion at my side. My lurcher, Dylan ... who is ten years old as I write this. His training, accomplished between puppy-hood and three years old was a long apprenticeship. My readers have shared the humour, frustration, often near-tragedy but mostly success that Dylan and I have enjoyed as a partnership. Those are stories for a future book. Over the years I have supplied myriad short articles to the country-sports press (and even chapters in my books) about how Dylan and I work together. I have finally succumbed to the many requests that I write a book on how I trained Dylan to work with the rifle.

Let say, before you start to read, that there are far better dog trainers about than me. Yet I have met few shooting men or women that have taken the time to ensure that the hound at their side is trained to perform in their own personal best interest or trained the dog to mirror their own personality. If the old adage about dogs being like their owners is true, then most shooters dogs I meet must be owned by hooligans! When I broke the rules to put a chasing dog at my side and then teach it not to chase, many folk frowned. Ten years on, many of those same folk look on enviously at the complete symbiosis achieved by a man, an air rifle and a scruffy old lurcher.

This book therefore, is not intended as a manual on training an obedience champion. It is a common-sense approach to producing a dog which behaves around a rifle ... any rifle ... and a rifleman or woman who behaves around a disciplined dog. Yes, in many ways, this book is about training the hunter ... not just the hound.

Ian Barnett
April 2014

OF MAN AND DOG

It is claimed that DNA proves that every domestic dog is descended from the wolf. Ever since canines were first domesticated they have been important partners in the development of the human race. Quite who domesticated who is probably open to debate? Rock paintings and hieroglyphics show us how ancient the relationship is. Archaeological excavations often turn up the remains of dogs clearly living in commune with humans. Personally, I think those early hounds must have been more cunning than we give them credit for. They obviously figured out that in following these tribes of awkward and uncouth half-apes, there was benefit. In return for guarding flocks or catching small game and dropping some at the humans feet they enjoyed shelter, fire, water and a share of the spoils. Humans, as they refined and developed, started to recognise this partnership to the point where they realised they could improve upon natures design of the canine with a bit of selective breeding. The purpose of dogs also changed in many ways. Across the millennia our hounds developed into various breeds for various purposes. Not least of these were the breeds that started to refine into the working and hunting lines we enjoy today. Retrievers, chasers, flushers, diggers, swimmers, jumpers, pointers, trackers .. even guards and killers. Dogs with genuine purpose kept by humans with a genuine purpose or need to own a dog.

The disciplined, experienced hunters hound is the hunters fifth limb. The acute sensory perception of the dog gives the hunter an extension of his or her hearing, scenting, sighting and even the 'sense' of compassion. Pointing and marking the proximity of live quarry, indicating incoming quarry, holding quarry at bay, retrieving dead (or, gently, live) quarry. Even tracking and helping mercifully despatch injured quarry. The hunters dog is a wonderful companion. Far more than merely a tool, the hunters dog is an extension of its owners hunting soul and ethos. A partner.

Of course, just as there are many breeds of hunting dog, so there are many types of hunting human. Bow hunters, ferreters, long-netters, deer stalkers, fox hunters, pack hunters, poachers, moochers, wild-fowlers, driven game shooters, trappers, pest controllers etc. Some need or prefer dogs in their company. Others don't need a dog.

This book narrows this list to those who hunt with a rifle, for reasons explained in the foreword. In particular, the hunter who stalks close to his or her quarry and needs a hound trained in stealth and silence.

WHAT TYPE OF DOG?

Let's start with the choice of dog. Unfortunately many shooters plunge into getting a dog without thinking carefully about what they want it to achieve. Just because a breed is badged as a 'gun-dog' doesn't mean it will work effectively to any type of gun. Basically, there are two types of hunting shooter, aren't there? The rifle / bow hunter and the shotgunner. Both need very different types of dog.

Shot-gunners, with the advantage of a scattered shot pattern, can take their quarry on the move. Even in flight. Therefore they need dogs that will quarter and flush, pushing game and quarry into movement. Having shot something, they want it retrieved, very often from water. Hence we have hyperactive, strong-willed little dogs like cocker or springer spaniels. Or they have stalwart recovery dogs like labradors or retrievers. Rifle shooters and bow hunters generally shoot static quarry. They get in close and want as little disturbance as possible. Their dogs need to be silent and extremely biddable, yet capable of scenting and finding, possibly retrieving when asked. It makes sense then to seek out a hound which has been bred for such tasks. That's why the deer stalker uses breeds such as Vizslas and German Wire-haired Pointers. But what of the air rifle hunter? The air-gunner has a wider choice but as the shooter who needs to get closest of all to their quarry, they need total obedience and silence. Spaniels and terriers, I would argue, are unsuitable due to their in-bred restlessness and inclination to 'talk'. Though I'm sure there will be many readers out there who would argue otherwise. Though my personal choice is the lurcher, I see no reason why a trainable dog like a labrador or border collie wouldn't work well to an air rifle.

So, why do I choose the lurcher? In a nutshell, history and romance .. and a lifetimes reliability from this mongrel 'breed'. I worked lurchers (loosely speaking a cross between any sighthound such as greyhound, whippet or saluki and a terrier or collie) long before I took the air rifle seriously. In my youth I was known to poach a rabbit and hare or two (I'm not confessing to too many!). Brought up on a fodder of books by Brian Plummer, Richard Jeffries and others who romanticised the black arts of the rural poacher, I saw myself as a throwback to the eighteenth century. That included walking the woods and fields with a catapult in my pocket and a gangly, broken-coated cur trotting alongside me. If the truth was known, had I not worked in a factory too I would have starved to death trying to live as a moocher! It was the air rifle that really started to fill my larder. Yet the use of a lurchers nose and ears became indispensable. Notwithstanding the pure joy of having a companion in the field that enjoys hunting as much myself and moulds its behaviour to my hunting style. Lurchers were bred by the old poachers and Romanies to run fast, run silent, nip over a fence at the flick of a finger to steal a chicken or lie low in cover at a whisper. The bigger lurchers could run down a deer, course a hare and snuff out a fox. All round hunting dogs which still exist today though their activities are sadly curtailed by ridiculous laws. The main trait, however, is that biddability. That absolute intelligence which allows them to absorb teaching quickly and to memorise through association, making them fast learners in the hunting field. That trait is bred into the bloodlines via the mongrelism. Pure sighthounds like whippets and greyhounds are superb chasers but (usually) difficult to train. Add a splash of terrier or collie blood and you add 'trainability'. In my Dylan's case, that comes from his whippet x Bedlington terrier father. His mother was a greyhound x deerhound.

Now, before everyone rushes out to get a lurcher I want to state three things, if you will allow? First of all, many air-gunners buy their gun and already own a dog. Please don't expect your old dog to suddenly adopt the behaviours needed to work at your new-found sport. Old dogs, new tricks? It's simply not fair on the dog. Secondly, don't abandon your loyal old hound to get a new dog just to work to the air-rifle. Having a dog at your side while air-gunning isn't essential. It helps (if they are trained well) but a dog is not a 'must-have' accessory. Thirdly, if you have room in your life and you are yearning for a dog, do not ever, ever consider a mature dog. The temptation may be there to take on a rescue dog or buy an allegedly 'trained to hunt everything' dog from the country-sports press. Just think carefully about this. With a rescue dog, you have no inkling of its history or actual breeding. As for the latter option, good hunters and dog trainers never sell a highly trained and reliable dog. Something is wrong.

It took me three years to get Dylan to the standard he is now. No amount of money could compensate for the time invested and loyalty we have to each other now. A dog trained to your own personal standard and behaviour is more than just a 'dog'. It is your guardian angel, your conscience, your guide and your companion. All of which means you need to start at the beginning, with a pup. But don't let that put you off. The end result will be _your_ dog. Nor will that dog, when you reach that level, work for anyone else in the same way as it does for you. It won't even behave, in general company, the way it does for you out in the field.

Whatever breed you choose, the training principles applied in this book should help to mould an efficient rifle hunting hound. If I was to pick out any essential traits for such a dog they would be lack of tongue (a dogs bark will empty the forest of nearby quarry in seconds) and a relaxed demeanour. Just give some thought for a minute on why 'lurchers' were so named? That lazy, loping, silent gait is hugely reminiscent of the hunting wolf. Wolves don't bark, either. Yet lurchers, like wolves, can transform in seconds into powerful and athletic predators.

Ultimately, choice of breed is a very personal decision. I wish you luck with your choice.

A Pup Comes Home

After a sabbatical from lurcher ownership, due to life changes I won't bore you with here, my new wife and I decided that our new home deserved a puppy. The debate started. Cheryl was from a shooting family and used to having labrador retrievers around. I wanted another lurcher. She wasn't really sure what a lurcher was. We were at an impasse until one day, strolling around Earlham Park in Norwich a huge, rangy and scruffy sight-hound unleashed a sprint across the rolling grassland. It coursed in wide sweeping circles, filling its lungs with air, jinking and turning on a sixpence, it's long tongue lolling. It ran back to its master and stood panting. My wife was captivated and asked me what it was? Was it a deerhound? I explained that it was a broken-coated, deerhound-cross lurcher. The seed was sown. Two weeks later, having seen a small ad in a local advertiser for a deerhound/greyhound x bedlington/whippet cross litter I made a phone call. Four pups left. Two dogs, two bitches. Did they have any broken-coated brindles? Yes, one bitch. Ok, I'll be there in two hours. The girl on the phone gave me some directions, an Irish lilt in her voice, and we set off for the Norfolk / Suffolk border.

Driving onto the site I drew in my breath. A tinker camp. The place was a mess. No house, just some ramshackle caravans, tied up horses and piles of scrap metal. We were about to back out and pass on looking at the litter when a large broken-coated deerhound/greyhound cross bitch loped up to the car and stood staring at me through the window. She was a beauty. My wife and I looked at each other. I suggested that if this was Mum, we'd better take a look at these pups. The girl I had spoken to on the phone came out to meet us. "I see you've met the mother!" she commented. As we walked past one of the caravans she pointed at a chained, dark coated bedlington/whippet. An older dog than the mother. "Thats the father" said our host. "We have to chain him 'cos he keeps stealing chickens from the farm down the road" she giggled. She couldn't possibly know it (nor could my wife) but she was saying all the right things. "The pups are round the back. They're probably ok now but they had a bit of a drama earlier". She patted the bitch, who was trotting along beside us. "Mum brought 'em a live hare earlier and jumped into the kennel with it. Let it go and jumped out again! Bleddy hare was bigger than the pups! Terrified them!" I was loving this, until I saw the 'kennel'. The pups were living outdoors inside a circle of straw bales with no shelter. The enclosure was filthy, full of faeces, no sign of food or water. The picture on Cheryls face told me that if I wasn't careful, we'd be leaving with four pups! I watched the pups, who all came to the wall of straw to greet us (probably hoping for food, though they didn't look underfed).

The brindle bitch wasn't broken coated at all, she was smooth coated. The other three pups pushed her away and scrabbled at the bales. I reached in and pulled her out and she lay trembling in my arms as I inspected her teeth, ears and claws. She couldn't make eye-contact. As I was doing this, I watched my wife who was leaning over the bales, talking to what was obviously the runt of the litter. A scruffy, full-coated ball of grey and white. As I held the brindle pup, which was as skittish as a deer faun, the runt ran an excited circle of the enclosure, sprinted towards its siblings, climbed up their backs and launched itself at my wife who caught it in her arms. It started licking at her face and as I watched her face light up I thought .. "Oh no!".

"Did you see that!" she asked. I couldn't lie. I had. She was cuddling the pup, who was still licking her face and hands. I slipped the timid brindle bitch back into the enclosure. "Cheryl .. It's white and grey!". That obviously didn't matter. "What sex is it?" The tinker girl answered. "He's a dog. Lovely isn't he? I was thinking of keeping him for myself!" I saw my wife hug him tighter and thought what a brilliant sales pitch the girl had just made. "Are these your dogs?" I asked. "No, Dads. He's back in Ireland buying some horses." I then tried a dangerous tactic. I've haggled for a few things in my time but to be honest they've never involved emotional wives and Irish horse traders. "The bitch is smooth-coated, you told me she was broken. She'll never make a hunter. Too timid. We've come a long way for nothing. I'll give you £100 for the dog." The girl put her hands on her hips. "It's £150, cash. Nothing wrong with that dog." I made to walk away and the tinker girl went to claim back the pup. I saw the plea in my wifes face. "Here. £150 cash". It ended amicably and I asked for a pic of the pups parents together, though all I had was a camera phone with a 3 megapixel camera.

On the drive back, Cheryl sat in the back of the motor hugging a trembling pup (first time in a motor vehicle). She announced that he was covered in fleas. No surprises there. My mind was elsewhere. This was not the dog I set out acquire and train. Perhaps we would end up with two lurchers? His and Hers dogs? We'd see.

Good Dog, Bad Dog?

An important factor in training your dog will be understanding right from wrong. Approval and disapproval. One thing I will guarantee you. For every good behaviour you train into your hound, everyone around you (especially your family) will be undoing that training unknowingly. Which is why I stand firmly by the Alpha / Beta principle when training a dog. My dog can behave erratically or inappropriately around friends or family and I will often turn a blind eye. Often, this includes defending the dog when it has over-stepped the mark. However, if I intervene and give a command, I expect implicit obedience. Alpha male. A perfect example will be that I never allow my lurcher to jump up at people. Can you imagine introducing him to a new landowner when I'm asking for shooting permission. Two muddy paws across the shoulders, a lick and a dog's breath kiss are hardly going to help my cause! Yet, the father-in-law will walk through the door and say 'Where's my Dylan?', clap his hands and encourage the dog to jump and greet him! Of course, when Nanny walks in .. five foot nothing and seven stone .. the dog greets her the same way and gets verbally slaughtered by everyone. So the poor dog doesn't know what he's done wrong while they're picking Nanny up off the floor! I'm sure we all know similar situations.

The important point here is that no matter how your dog behaves around the rest of your 'pack' .. sorry, family but that's how he sees you .. you must maintain Alpha male or female status and keep your dog in check. So how do you do that? Here's a tip. Watch a few wildlife documentaries about big cats or wild dog packs. What you witness may surprise you with its simplicity.
The unruly youngster in a wild pack is tolerated lightly by the Alpha leader, yet rarely hurt. Dominance and education is achieved through mild rebuke, visible disapproval and (very often)disdain. Just like children looking for attention through bad behaviour, ignoring such behaviour can often work better than constant reprimand.

When you imprint Alpha status over a pup .. and only you can do that .. it will just want please you. A pup will become quite agitated if you ignore it or disown it. So that's how to show disapproval at bad behaviour. Not beating the dog, shutting it out or starving it. That will only ever serve to instil fear and mistrust. Reaction to bad behaviour needs to be instant, associative and must show in your own body language and voice. Each instance needs to be dealt with individually so it's difficult to generalise here, though I will try to give some examples.

You are teaching the pup to fetch a ball and release it to your hand but it keeps trying to retain the ball and bites you when you try free the ball. You should react immediately with a loud 'Bad!' and turn away from the play. Walk away, do something else, ignore the pup. Game over today. Do this every time it bites. Don't hit the dog, nor wrestle the ball from its grip. The wrestle becomes the game, not the retrieve, so needs to be discouraged. If you hit the pup, why would it want to retrieve again? Make a huge fuss of the dog when it releases the ball. It will soon associate right behaviour from wrong.
You are heel training the pup off-lead on a country track. It keeps ranging too far ahead. You call it to heel but it ignores you. Don't shout at it. It will note your anger and will be reluctant to come back to you. Instead, just mutter 'Bad!' and turn back. Walk back towards where you started. When it comes back to follow you (and it usually will) praise it, say 'heel' and start again.

You may be stock training, perhaps walking the pup on a lead through a flock of ducks. It can't resist attempting a snap at one of the birds. You tug firmly on the lead, saying 'Bad!' very firmly while engaging eye contact with the pup. When you reach the point where the dog trots obediently through the flock beside without trying to bite the stock, you praise the pup generously. Can you see the point I am making here? That the pup needs education, not discipline. Disapproval .. in your actions (walking away, dis-owning), your voice (as with the low growl of the dam or sire) and in your facial expression (the scowl, the stoney eyes) .. all imitate the way the pup would be treated in a pack environment. Resorting to violence against your dog does nothing to encourage good behaviour, trust or bonding. It simply demonstrates a lack of self-control or mis-understanding of your dogs psychological needs.

I mentioned 'biting' above for good reason. It is an anti-social behaviour which, in this day and age, simply must not be encouraged or tolerated. Play-biting is natural in a puppies development, particularly when teething, but mustn't be allowed to exceed 'play' levels. Nor would any sensible hunter want to encourage a hard mouth on their hound. When it learns to retrieve, you want the pup to bring back edible game or fowl .. not a mouthful of mincemeat! The best way to deal with over exuberant biting in a pup is to immediately chastise with 'Bad!' and that angry scowl.

General Good Manners

Like your children, how your dog behaves in your home may not hold great importance to you. It does to me (both the children and the dogs!). The hunters hounds general behaviour in the field will make or break the hunters impression on other hunters (and landowners). A well-behaved, disciplined and obedient dog reflects highly on the hunters own self-discipline and dedication to his or her sport. Training-in etiquette is an important part of your pups overall learning (and your own claim to be a responsible dog owner) so if you get it right, your dog will be as welcome as you around field and farm. So let's take a look at basic etiquette. Strange as it may seem to you, a dog owner, not everyone likes your dog. There are still an amazing amount of folk who fear dogs, of any breed. Therefore two behaviours worth curbing in your dog are barking and jumping-up to greet people.

Barking

Yes .. I'm afraid I'm one of those people who buys a dog and barks himself! Silence in a rifle hunters dog is imperative, which is why I choose the lurcher as a companion. Yet even they bark sometimes. Dogs generally bark when they are excited, frightened or frustrated. Just think about that for a moment? Encouraging a pup to bark at home or around people may seem amusing at the time but out in the field it could destroy the silent stalk you seek to achieve with your rifle. One particular manifestation of this is, which I have experienced, is the dog voicing its frustration at departing quarry such as squirrels or rabbits. Once a dog starts this it becomes a habit hard to break, so as far a rifle-mans dog is concerned, the dog is ruined .. and if you keep it at your side, so is your effectiveness as a stalker.
Curbing the barking habit early in a pup isn't hard at all. You need to be prepared, though, to watch the pup carefully and to use some shock tactics. Pups dislike sudden noise so having a small tin of ball-bearings to hand is a good ploy. The game here is not to let the pup know you are responsible

for the noise. When the pup starts to give voice, rattle the tin loudly. Keep doing this until the pup associates the fright with the barking. Another method some use is a squirt from a water pistol. Again, the pup mustn't see you do it.

Jumping Up

Your dog jumping up at people, particularly with a large hound, can either deter visitors (you might actually want this if you are a sociopath) or make you unwelcome on others land. Your Vizla or lurcher standing up to place two muddy paws on the shoulders of the shoot captains £1000 tweed jacket and planting a sloppy, dog-breath tongue in his face is hardly going to guarantee you an invitation next time! Nor is flattening the farmers young daughter in a cow-squit covered yard. This sort of behaviour is best curbed while the dog is on the lead, including slipping a lead on just before letting people into your home or visiting. The old gamekeepers had a way of handling a dog that jumped up at them persistently and that was stand on one of its back paws heavily. I'm sure a hound would quickly lose the habit given such short, sharp treatment but there is a risk that the dogs toe could be broken, ruining it. Training should never need excessive force so it's not a method I would advocate.

Toilet Manners

On the subject of manners, another way to lose favour with friends and peers is to disregard your dog when it defecates or urinates in company. Please don't assume that because you're in the muster-yard and there are other dogs are about that you can ignore the steaming pile your hound has just deposited under the tailgate of the landowners Range Rover. Carry a bag and clear up. Better that than facing the humiliation of the 'his Lordship' handing you his Hunter boots and saying "Now be a good chap and clean your dogs crap off my boots, there's a good fellow!"

Begging

Begging for and (worse still) stealing food is another habit to stop in its tracks. This is another behaviour which rarely starts of the dogs own volition. It is usually started and encouraged by the family. With due respect to pocket-treats, which are a useful training aid, try to keep the dog eating from its bowl. There is nothing more annoying than a dog pestering people at their food, particularly house guests.

Aggression

If your hound has a pugilistic nature (remember, it's often said that dogs are like their owners!) then you need to ensure it can't harm other dogs when in their company. This may mean muzzling young Tyson until he's working. Though when working, you will need to keep a close eye on a canine thug as dogs are at their most unpredictable when they are jealous or feel possessive. Personally, I wouldn't accept any type of constant aggression in a dog … any more then I would in a human. Not my ideal company, which is why I incline to passive breeds like the lurcher.

Very few pups are born with behavioural aberrations. There may be aggression in-built through breeding but it is rarely directed at the pups parents or owner unless wrongly encouraged. Freud for dogs? You bet. If an older dog has behaviour problems, you can bet a human was involved somewhere in its early years. Dogs themselves make resolute parents so they don't screw up their puppies minds. Humans do. Another very good reason for refusing an adult dog and starting out with a puppy.

You will occasionally come across a pup, particularly a dog pup, that seeks to test your Alpha status and see how far it can push its luck. This is particularly true in a dogs 'adolescence' when it is trying to adjust to sexual maturity. In your dog, this about twenty to thirty months old. Just like the pouting human teenager, you may experience some testing of your authority and wisdom. Dylan certainly went through this stage and a large dog like a lurcher starting to snap and snarl can be intimidating for the whole family. Thankfully I had the experience to quell this trait quickly, based on a technique I had read somewhere in my youth and had used before. This a firm, safe way to neutralise aggressive behaviour and I would recommend any dog owner to adopt this simple exercise anyway, while the pup is young. When the dog is being boisterous, hold its collar and step across its back as if you were going to ride it. Quickly place one arm under its chest, right behind the fore-legs, with the other still holding its collar firmly. Lift the dogs front paws off the floor and hug it tightly. It may struggle, may even try to turn it's head to snap at you .. but it can do little if you are holding it firmly. If it does struggle, keep it up in this position until it ceases. Talk gently to it, 'Good boy or girl', until it settles. Lower the dog slowly. If it starts to wrestle, don't release it. Lift it again. Keep doing this until the dog accepts that you are in control. Don't let the dog win the 'wrestling' match. If it does, it's won. You might as well go sleep in dog basket! This exercise should be repeated frequently during the dogs life. I honestly believe that older dogs take some comfort from this confirmation of status. Oh .. and another tip. If any of your other 'pack members' (i.e. the kids) are being bullied by the pup get them to do the same, though strictly under your supervision. It goes without saying that you mustn't let four year old Emily try this with your Rhodesian Ridgeback! This is an exercise for the Alpha adult with a challenging, not dangerously vicious, dog. Where does this come from, psychologically? Watch a bitch with young pups and how she checks misbehaviour. She picks them up by the scruff. Cats do the same, particularly big cats. If you use this technique, use it often .. even when showing affection to your dog. It just serves as a gentle reminder of who holds the power.

Socialisation

During its lifetime, your dog will hopefully be sharing a very varied life with you. It will go shopping, be taken on holiday, and attend game-fairs (perhaps even be entered in shows). Ensuring your dog is sociable is down to you. The more contact you give your pup with people and other dogs, the easier it will find these encounters and understand what behaviour is acceptable. Dylan loves big social occasions whereas I hate them. That may be because he gets so much attention, being such an unusual colour. I've told this story a few times now but it's worth repeating here. We were at the East Anglian Gamefair a few years back and I was standing alongside a stand where my wife was shopping. An old chap was standing staring at us. His wife walked up to him and he pointed across to us. "There's that Dylan from the magazines ... with that bloke!", he commented.

Car Etiquette

Many of us will travel to hunt and keep our dogs in the tailgate of an estate, pickup or 4x4. I always ensure that the dog has something soft to lie on (particularly on long journeys). I carry water and a first aid kit. I've never needed to use a cage for a dog as I always ensure the dog is trained very early to stay in the tailgate until invited out. This is a sensible discipline for myriad reasons, some of which are explained elsewhere in this book. The main reason, however, is pure control and containment. When I arrive on someone else's land (whether joining company or not) my dog isn't invited out of the car until I've checked it's safe, we won't disturb game or livestock unexpectedly and there is no threat from traffic. If someone comes up to chat with me I will send the dog to lie in the open tailgate while we talk. If they want to make a fuss of him (many folk do) I call him out. Again (and I won't apologise for repeating this many times in this book) a hunter who can demonstrate total control of their dog (s) will be welcomed, often admired, by most farmers and landowners. An unruly dog only serves to indicate an unruly owner.

Body Language

In my 'day job', in my role as a people-manager, interpretation of body language and a very basic understanding of psychology has always been a prerequisite of my success (or failure). So why wouldn't I apply those same techniques in 'managing' a dog? It makes perfect sense. Understanding if your dog is happy, sad, worried, ill, fearful, skittish or angry are important not just to the animal but also to anyone interacting with it.

Cast your mind back to the chapter 'Man and Dog' earlier. Underneath that skin and fur your hound has the distant genetic make-up of a wolf. Our human intervention has done nothing but confuse the domestic canine psyche over thousands of years of anthropomorphising one of nature's most efficient predators. In some dogs, the line between domesticity and savagery is so thin it can be breached seriously through cruelty, neglect or misunderstanding. In most cases it won't be the dogs fault, it will be human behaviour (or most likely, mis-behaviour) that is the root cause of a dog 'gone wrong'. Hence the need to read any dogs body language before judging it.

The Tail That Wags The Dog

My old Dad (who hated dogs only because he feared them) used to tell me that you shouldn't approach a dog whose tail isn't wagging. There is much truth in that old chestnut but the dog may have stopped wagging its tail for a few reasons. The tail of a dog could be considered a pretty useless appendage except for balance when running and turning at speed. Yet those who know dog behaviour well will confirm that the tail is a mirror of the dogs heart and soul. Just as we humans draw in all muscles tightly when we fear something ... the brace reaction ... dogs lower their head, pull back the ears, draw in the neck and curl the tail underneath the body. If someone approaches a dog and it does it this, it is scared of them. If you see the owner of a dog approach it and it cowers like this, I'll lay a thousand pounds you're looking at a cruel owner.

The strongly wagging tail is synonymous with a happy dog, for sure, so should be used to gauge a dogs temperament ... but be careful! It isn't necessarily synonymous with good behaviour. The pup that has just pulled the Sunday beef joint off the kitchen worktop and eaten it will be wagging its tail frantically! Nor should you assume that a dog with the tail between its legs is going to be aggressive. Quite the opposite. It is being submissive and cautious. If you approach humbly, lower yourself to the dogs eye level and talk gently that tail will probably start to wag. That tail between the legs posture is going to be important to remember as you train your pup. When you catch the pup eating the Sunday beef joint (you will if you pick a lurcher and turn your back too long!) you will reprimand it with firm words, a dominant posture and a wag of the finger. No more than that. When the pup looks at you dolefully, neck down and tail between its legs, it has understood your sermon. The dog knows it has displeased you and has reacted with the only apology it is capable of. Submission.

The signal, in the dogs tail, to be wary of is the outstretched, erect and still tail. The same posture that your hunting dog, in maturity, will adopt when it marks quarry or is about to launch a sprint at quarry. Eyes staring, ears erect, tail horizontal. That posture, in a social situation, needs to be taken seriously. Particularly if the dog is being pestered by children, which it will usually only consider as siblings, not 'humans'. No matter how precious you think your kids are, to the family dog they may be just other pups vying for your attention.

THE TALE OF TWO DOGS

I saw this on Facebook, author unknown, so thought it was a parable worth repeating here.
There is a story they tell of two dogs.
Both at separate times walk into the same room.
One comes out wagging his tail while the other comes out growling.
A woman watching the two dogs walks into the room to see what could possibly make one dog so happy and the other so mad?
To her surprise, she finds a room filled with mirrors.
The happy dog found a thousand happy dogs looking back at him.
While the angry dog saw only angry dogs growling back at him.
What you see in the world around you is a reflection of who you are.

THE EYES HAVE IT

Part of the training regime of a young pup will involve play-hunting. Throwing old balled up socks to retrieve. Natural instinct (that wolf thing again) will see the pup ragging its catch, swinging it about, pinning it down, delivering the killer bite. Your socks are officially dead. Watch the pups eyes throughout this play. They are wide, gleaming, attentive ... until that killer bite. Just before the 'strike' the pupils will narrow as the lips curl back over the pups lips to bare the teeth that are its only weapon. The tail will be still and it will pounce, viciously. The whole scenario will last just five seconds, perhaps less. Trust me, you want this type of body language in the hunting field and in training. So please don't mistake it for social aggression. That is one reason the hunter must also 'train' the family not to compete with the dog in chase and play games. If a dog is encouraged to wrestle for a fetched object within its jaws, expect to be bitten. In fact, if it's my dog, I hope he does bite you! Because until given a release command, the object is his, by right. Check the eyes, though. My lurcher will grip but won't wrestle. His soft eyes will tell you he's playing. Waiting for the command to release. Try to force the release (grab his nose or try to lever the object from his lips) and his eyes will narrow and harden. A low growl will build.
The grip of his teeth will tighten. Time to back off ... or in my case simply utter "Dead"! Yet imagine that the protagonist was a five year old child and a dog less disciplined than mine?

BAD HEALTH SIGNALS

Other than vocal signals (whining and wittering) we often have few indications of our hounds health other than its body language. Most dog owners will be aware of the normal physical 'carriage' of their dog (how it walks, runs, lies, sits, eats, etc). All of these can be acute indicators of our dogs health (or lack of). A dog carrying its neck low often indicates a throat or mouth problem. If the hound has dug burrs from its paws or coat and swallowed some of the barbs they will catch on the tongue and in the throat causing soreness and irritation. Persistent coughing should be taken seriously as it could signal a number of illnesses including parvo-virus or kennel cough. A hound carrying its back legs stiffly may be showing signs of hip dysplasia or it could simply be blocked anal glands. If the dog is scraping its backside on the floor you can bet it has worms. Check its stools for signs. All dogs should be wormed regularly and treated for other parasites like fleas and ticks. This is even more important in hunting dogs who spend a great deal of time exposed to nematode or tapeworm eggs and to ticks, fleas and lice.

Dogs will also exhibit the sort of obvious physical signals that we do which indicate ill health. Runny nose, weeping eyes, limps, itches, rumbling stomach. What they can't do is actually tell us what's hurting. I'm not a fan at all of DIY diagnosis or curatives. If you think it's serious, get your dog to a vet. I would remind you too, at this point, that it is against the law to allow an animal to suffer and to attempt surgery without the requisite qualifications. That includes stitching a wound.

Dogs And The Weather

Behaviour in many animals and birds can be influenced by the weather, as I've written in my other books. Dogs aren't an exception to this but like humans, their reaction to various weather conditions varies between individuals rather than breeds. Take thunder, for instance. My dog can stand next to a shotgun range all day without flinching but a short rumble of thunder will see him cowering and whimpering, looking for somewhere to hide. By reading his body language I know when a storm is close enough for me to head for cover, even before the first flash of lightning or thunder-crack. The major reasons for understanding your dog's body language in relation to weather though will be to monitor its health in hot or cold conditions. I'm no 'fair weather' hunter. I love to be outdoors, so Dylan often accompanies me in extreme cold or in searing heat and I watch his demeanour very carefully in both. As a hunter, you have to ... for your dog's own prey-drive will often cause it to battle on when it is in great discomfort. In hot conditions the lolling tongue, heavy panting and constant seeking of shade to lie in should tell you it's time to quit and find shade and water for the animal. In extreme cold, if the dog starts to shiver uncontrollably get it into the warm quickly. In snow, watch for balling of ice between the dogs toes. Pull them out rather than let them thaw out, which can be agony for the dog.

ALIEN ENCOUNTERS

No, I don't mean X-Files type stuff. I mean those encounters which clearly frighten a dog for no obvious reason. I have no idea why but Dylan has an absolute terror of hot air balloons. During warm weather we get a fair bit of balloon traffic across our area. If he's in the garden he can sense a balloon approaching while it is still two miles away. He must be able to either hear the burner or smell the fuel it uses. He will skulk up and down, whining and wittering, watching the skies. At first sight of a balloon he will growl and run indoors to hide behind a sofa or a bed. If we're walking we need to leash him quickly as he has bolted for home in the past. The only theory I have around this absurd phobia is that the tinker camp where we bought him was next to a dis-used RAF airfield often used to launch and land balloons so perhaps he associated them with those first twelve weeks of life amongst the hay bales?

HOMING, FEEDING AND EXERCISE

Here we come to the first few lessons for the hunter, not the dog!

Referring back to a comment I made earlier, bonding with a pup is (in my humble opinion) far better achieved by the rifleman if the dog is kept close and not kennelled. You will be asking for a level of discipline from your hound that surpasses the 'mooching pack' and I definitely don't mean any detriment in that statement. In my case, knowing that I was going to ask my pup to overcome many of his natural instincts, I needed absolute implicit trust from day one. This surprises many people, as I have a very laissez-faire attitude to my guns. To me, they are simply tools. Sure, they need to be maintained, cleaned and oiled. I know many shooters who treat their guns like goddesses yet treat their hounds with complete disdain. Guns are ten-a-penny. A loyal, trained dog is absolutely priceless. The relationship between hunter and dog needs to be damn near as close as husband and wife (I need to be careful here, in case my wife buys a Kindle!) yet you need to maintain that Alpha / Beta status too.

I won't even attempt to relay house training techniques here. These are so basic, and explored in other books by standard trainers, that it would be insulting. Though I will stop here to say that if a dog is to share your home, this is essential training. I don't just mean hygiene training. To maintain that Alpha / Beta status there must be ground rules. The dog should be aware of these. Simple rules such as where the dog lies, sleeps, sits. How it behaves when you eat (no begging or scavenging). Where the dog eats (from its bowl .. not off your plate!). Sleeping arrangements should be firm. A bed in the corner ... not the family sofa!

I knew from previous experience that the best way to bond with a dog is in the way that the old poachers used to, so Dylan (as with all my past dogs) was never kennelled. He is a house dog. Moochers of old used to let their dogs sleep close by, even on their bed. No, I don't go that far! The fact that I was going to train this pup to over-ride some his most primal instincts meant that we had to bond implicitly and I had to gain his complete confidence. Believe me when I say that over the next year that relationship was to be sorely tested on many occasions (by both sides) until we reached the mutual understanding necessary to work in harmony in the field. Another golden rule is the same as that I apply to my guns. The more you work with just one rifle, the better your proficiency becomes. So for me, like the old poachers, a simple policy applies. One dog, total focus. I'm sure the gamekeepers of the past knew, beware the man with one lurcher!

How we feed our dogs is often dictated by lifestyle and the dogs own preference. From pup to middle age, Dylan was on a BARF diet (bone and raw food). For some reasons he suddenly started to decline bone content and we switched to feeding him ready mixed raw meats and vegetables (a brand called Natures Menu is excellent). I always mix this with some moist cereal mix (Norfolk Gold is a preference). Much as I would love to process his food from our own shooting gains (rabbit, squirrel and pigeon) I simply don't have time. With a full time day job, a long commute either way and my writing I use my spare time wisely (hunting!). As I often cook rabbit and pigeon in one form or other, the dog gets its fair share of prime natural meat whenever I do. I also have no qualms in feeding cooked leftovers such as chicken or beef ... but always in his bowl, mixed with his normal food. As my lurchers ageing stomach can't cope with bone I treat him to roasted pig ears and jerky chews to keep his teeth clean. One of the key things to remember when feeding your dog is that they like variety, just like us.

Any dog needs exercise (and it does us no harm either). The amount or type of exercise will be different from breed to breed. I do read some nonsense at times about lurchers and greyhounds needing two five-mile walks a day to stay fit. All I can say is that who-ever writes such advice doesn't do an honest days work! Exercise also needs to be quality rather than quantity where possible. For the rifle-man there has to be a balance between keeping a sharp edge of speed in the dog but also stamina. My dog may be in the field for hours and hours but rarely break above a trot. Should I need his help to dispatch, I want speed. Yet unlike (for example) a lamping lurcher which runs down the beam to snatch up live, jinking, sprinting rabbits, my dog needs no such speed. Thus when I exercise him, I want it to stretch his brain as much as his muscle. For that reason, I try to exercise off-lead and in-country as much as possible. Of course, he has to endure the dark winter trot on the lead around under fog-shrouded street-lights from time to time. These low days can be complemented with diverse exercise at weekends. I'm lucky enough to live within an hours drive of the coast and a couple hours around the marram dunes and on the beach are superb free-running exercise for a dog.

A Pup Settles In

Bringing the new pup from a life outdoors into a house is always going to be interesting. One of the funniest moments I recall on that first night was the pups first experience of stairs. We just let the pup follow us about as he got used to surroundings and at one point, we were both upstairs and heard him squeaking below. We encouraged him up and he climbed cautiously. A lurcher pup at 12 weeks has gangly legs like a deer faun. The problem then was that he couldn't muster the courage to come back down when we did! Somewhere we have a wonderful photo of a doleful looking puppy, head between paws, gazing down the stairwell. It didn't take long, however, for curiosity to overcome fear. It is a good sign, from a training point of view, when your pup cannot bear to be out of your sight right from the start.

The first couple of nights were painful, as always. Not worrying the about abandoned pup crying below in the kitchen where it had water, a warm bed and a carpet of old newspaper. The first nights without either mother or siblings are traumatic for a puppy. The painful bit was restraining my wife from going to the pups rescue! It is vastly important that the puppy quickly learns to trust its own company and that you will return to it when the time is right. If the pup starts to associate pitiful bleating with a human coming to its aid, you will make hell for yourself. That's not theory. It's fact and one which a lot of human parents would do well to learn too!

Picking a name for a dog is always a recipe for contention, particularly in a family environment. For the hunter this actually quite important. Every command you give your dog in the early months is best 'trained-in' using its name in association. For instance "Dylan. Sit!" The name catches the dogs attention and it knows the command is directed at him. Thus, a simple single or two syllable name is best for both you and the hound. "Montgomery, lie down!" would become a tad tedious. "Monty, drop!" is far easier. We wanted a Gaelic / Celtic name to reflect the pups deerhound blood and settled on Dylan. Strangely, though I could have shortened it to 'Dyl' during training, I never did. Whereas my wife, who doesn't hunt, often calls him Dyl!

House training was the usual balance of diligence, guiding the pup to the door, several piles of old newspapers and a few bottles of disinfectant before the penny dropped. Dylans next big trauma was getting used to the fact that both my wife and I worked and that life wasn't one long 'weekend'. I wish!
Luckily Cheryl worked locally, so the pup was only left for a few hours at a time as she could get home for lunch.

Training started immediately with the basics such as sit, get here etc. Dylans world was quickly expanded from house to garden. After innoculations, lead training started and he was very responsive though Dylan became a bit heavy on the lead as he grew. This was soon checked (see the lead training section). We had picked him up in September and so much of his walking and initial training was done under street-lights both before and after work. At weekends, I spent as much time as possible with him though never out with a gun. He wouldn't be ready for that until he reached nine months old.

As his bones strengthened and his muscle definition grew, I spent hours walking and running him. Teaching him to chase, search for and retrieve dummies, jump to a reasonable height and behave around stock. His domestic behaviour was testing as it always will be with a teething, mentally developing canine. We had to write off a carpet or two, keep him away from the letterbox and thanks the heavens that we hadn't re-newed the furniture (which was planned before we decided to get a pup but put on hold)! By the way, before you buy a pup, you may want to read the section 'Indoor Behaviour'. At nine months I introduced Dylan to the world of hunting and airguns. By now, as he had been so responsive, all thought of my ideal dogs sex, colouration or coat had been long forgotten. In fact, as many of my book and magazine readers will testify, Dylans distinctive colouring and coat were to make him more instantly recognisable than his owner!

As if purposely challenging my branding of him as being 'the litter runt', Dylan soon developed into the best airgun hunting dog I could ever hope to own. I hope that Dylan, in his own account, would say that the feeling is mutual. I taught this dog everything I could to make him efficient. And he has taught me a hell of a lot along the way too.

Some Basic Training Rules

By basic, I mean the minimum level training any dog owner should seek to apply in order to keep the dog safe and make it 'socially' acceptable. Between three months and nine months old, Dylan rarely saw a rifle. Walking, exercising and training were geared around teaching him the important commands that keep a dog out of trouble.

Alpha / Beta Principles

One of the first principles of successful dog training is undoubtedly recognising the pack mentality of any hound and the Alpha / Beta hierarchy which is dominant in wild dog packs. In any pack, one male and/or female dominate. The Alpha hounds. The rest of the pack is subservient to these, often reliant on them for direction and leadership. In your relationship with your hunting hound it is vital that you adopt this Alpha animal status. In the wild and in your household, there will be occasions when other dogs challenge your Alpha status. That is a totally normal, natures way, so you need to learn how to assert yourself without resorting to brutality. Firm but fair is the rule. If this starts with puppy training you will see only a few, mild challenges along the way. There is an important point to note here. The puppy will see its status in the pack hierarchy as only marginally below that of your children, if you have any. So here's one of my first tips. Treat your dog as you do your children and you won't go far wrong. You wouldn't beat or chain your kids, I hope. Nor would you leave them hungry, thirsty, cold or put them in direct danger of harm. Give your dog, as you do your kids, as much attention, time and love as you can afford. That's not being soppy. It's being sensible. The way to get a highly efficient hunting dog is to get it to bond closely and completely trust you. It needs to respect you and want to be with you. But it needs to understand its place in the pack hierarchy and when it does, it will be quite happy. The developing pup needs to know when it has done wrong and when it has pleased you. More on that later.

I knew from previous experience that the best way to bond with Dylan was in the way that the old poachers used to, so Dylan was never kennelled. He is a house dog. Moochers and poachers of old used to let their dogs sleep close by, even on their bed. No, I didn't go that far! The fact that I was going to train this pup to over-ride some his most primal instincts meant that we had to bond implicitly and I had to gain his complete confidence. Believe me when I say that over the early years that relationship was to be sorely tested on many occasions (by both sides) until we reached the mutual understanding necessary to work in harmony in the field, but you will hear about that later.

The One-Dog Principle

Another golden rule is the same as that I apply to my guns. The more you work with just one rifle, the better your proficiency becomes. So for me, like the old poachers, a simple policy applies. One dog, total focus. I'm sure the gamekeepers of the past knew, beware the man with one lurcher. Though I may bring a young pup on behind Dylan in his dotage, to gain from his knowledge, I believe that two's company and three's a crowd. On the very rare occasions I allow someone to accompany me air-gun hunting, their dogs are banned. Which raises a few very important points about training a hunting dog. You are training your hound to work with you, no-one else. So don't even think about taking it to training 'classes'! If you're not prepared to spend the one-to-one time needed to help your dog understand what you want from him and what he needs from you, forget it. Go buy some budgies and sell your rifles. On the same theme, consider the training environment. Puppies, like children (and old air-gun writers!) have very short concentration spans. Train where there will be minimal or no distraction. Avoid public parks or farmyards. You will definitely want to use these later to test your success, but for those crucial one-to-one early sessions keep to your garden (dismissing the family) or a quiet meadow somewhere. Wherever you are, keep training sessions short. Boredom and disinterest will stifle a pups enthusiasm. Whatever you are teaching or encouraging should stop just as the pup reaches its height of excitement. This imprints on the brain. Between three months and nine months old, Dylan rarely saw a rifle. Walking, exercising and one-to-one training were geared around teaching him the three important commands that keep a dog out of trouble. Sit, recall (come back) and stay. Plus the basic 'play' training that helps develop a dogs fieldcraft. Fetching and finding.

THINK LIKE A DOG

Not as strange a concept as you may first consider, because you will soon discover that your dog constantly tries to think like a human! In my earlier hunting books I have always advocated that to match your quarry, you need to think like your quarry. Get into it's psyche. Dog training is similar. It becomes much simpler if you cross the barrier and try to imagine what's going on in the mind of that little tyke of a pup you've just let into your life. Anticipation of your pups likely behaviour (or mis-behaviour) and therefore acting to intervene in a positive way is one the key features in not only successfully training a hunting companion but also in bonding with your dog. Over a few years, as you have learned to think like your dog, it will also learn to think like you. So what am I suggesting when I say think like your dog? People who live around dogs regularly in a domestic environment probably know exactly what I mean. If you've raised house lurchers, you know not leave the chicken to defrost on the kitchen worktop! If you have a terrier, you don't turn over the vegetable patch and leave it outside, unwatched. It will be half-way to the earths core by the time you return! Training a pup in the hunting field is no different. Particularly when you've reached that point when you trust it just enough to let it range off-lead. At that point, you really do need to preempt what your dog will do and be ready to handle the consequences.

Thinking like a dog also means 'imagining' like a dog. Seeing the world around you from the dogs perspective. Yep .. I really do mean 'the dogs eye view'. When you're both out in the fields and woods you (with your high field of view, some five feet off the ground) can see things that your dog can't. Traffic, hazards, livestock, the rabbits you're hunting, the forbidden pheasant skulking into cover, the farm cat. You get the idea. You can prevent disaster and mishap by 'seeing' for your dog. When you see those rabbits, beyond the marram grass or nettle bed, remember that your dog can't see them. He may be able to smell them, but he can't see them. It's up to you to silently check his progress and take the shot. If you don't check him and he blunders through the foliage and scatters your quarry, it wasn't his fault!

Often, the concept of thinking like your dog means trusting its instincts and senses implicitly. Very often I will stand at the fork of woodland ride trying to decide which way to walk and my old hound will set off down one path and throw a knowing look over his shoulder as if saying 'Come on, this way Boss!' He is rarely wrong. On the other hand, be prepared for minor conflict if you have an agenda he doesn't understand. Don't reprimand the dog but don't allow rebellion either. I'll give you a simple example. One of the hunting tricks I give in my other books is to flush rabbits from a standing crop by deliberately working yourself and your dog so that your scent is carried on the breeze straight to the hiding quarry. This can panic them and make them bolt for the safety of their burrows. Many will pause on the field margin when they exit the crop cover, your chance to shoot them. Working a dog down the breeze is totally alien to its instinct, specially if it scents rabbits hiding up the breeze! Even after years of doing this in sugar beet crops, my lurcher has to be coaxed down the breeze. Respect that confusion. Think like your dog.

Think like your dog when you encounter the unusual. The rabbit put up at your feet that bolts across the road? Act quickly to stop pursuit. The 'anti' thundering towards you in an aggressive manner as you carry your rabbits back to your vehicle. Your dog will sense that aggression long before you and seek to protect you, which could spell disaster. Slip the lead on the dog. Thinking like your dog also means understanding its canine psyche and genetic desire to please you to the extent that you need, often, to put a check on these traits. A loyal dog will, literally, run itself into the ground for a good master or mistress. Be aware of that and never ask too much of your hound. Respect its age, ability, capability and stamina. Know when it needs water, rest, food, shade or first aid

The Training 'Commands'

An important point to make here is that despite my constant reference to 'commands' I rarely shout at my dog aggressively. I talk, firmly, or simply whisper. The word 'command' is indicative of control so I think it's a fair description of any words given to encourage the hunters dog to behave in a manner it should associate with that instruction

'Sit'

The sit command is hugely important (in Dylans case that was actually a 'drop' command as lurchers find sitting uncomfortable). This needs to be taught until it becomes automatic as it will, even from a distance, stop your dog in its tracks and bring it to the floor.

Beyond house-training, the 'sit' command is the one most commonly taught first to a puppy and is fairly easily encouraged during lead training. This is probably the first instruction you will give that can cause a dog to stop doing what it wants to do. A restraining instruction. Any commands of this nature are best taught on an obey / reward basis. One way to encourage a pup to sit back is to offer the treat just above its head, between the ears. It will naturally sit back and raise its muzzle to seek the reward. As it does so, simply say 'sit'. Walking the pup on a lead, as you reach a kerb or gateway pull back gently on the lead signalling the dog to stop and give the sit command while gently pushing down on the pups rump. If / when the pup responds by sitting, make a fuss of it and perhaps offer a small treat as a reward. Over a period of time, extend the duration of the 'sit' before rewarding. The dog needs to understand that the 'sit' means remain seated until released ('get on').

Be conscious of your dogs breed and its ability to sit comfortably though. Long legged hounds find the position uncomfortable due to the way their hips are angled. So, if you are pausing for some time (for instance, to chat to a neighbour) lie the dog instead. Similarly, don't ask a dog to sit for long on snow, frost, mud or wet ground. In these circumstances use the 'wait' command, which I will cover later.

Initially you will find that the pup may try to cheat to get the reward. It's rump will barely touch the ground and it will be up again, tail wagging, expecting a treat. Repeat the command and push gently on its rump again and again until the penny drops. If the pup refuses to sit, walk back a few paces, turn and return to where you gave the command. Try again. Keep doing this until the pup realises that until it obeys, the walk has stopped there.

The sit command can be encouraged off-lead at home at any time, though don't overdo it. Make sure the dog associates obedience with praise or reward and disobedience with disapproval. Practice getting the pup to sit at a distance from you in the garden and go to it with a reward. Soon you will be able to do this when the dog is off-lead, exercising. This and the recall command will become your invisible leash .. the one which will keep your dog out of trouble .. when your hound is some distance from you.

The sit command is the first one you will teach which also needs a release command. With a hunting hound, you will develop a few versions of this. 'Get on' or 'walk on' or, perhaps, 'come on'. These are so important, particularly in the pups learning and development. Too many people spend hours teaching a pup to sit but neglecting to teach the release. The result being a very confused puppy. It knows that to sit is what you expect but it doesn't know when to get up and follow you. If it gets up too early, it may get reprimanded. If it doesn't get up, it may get reprimanded. It's urge will be to move but it only wants to with your Alpha approval. So .. always remember to release the dog from any restraining command, even when on the lead.

'Get On' or 'Go On'

This is, quite simply, my release command. If you give your dog a restrictive instruction such as 'stay' or 'wait' it is unfair to expect them to work out when the command has expired. Your dog is trying to please you, so it needs to know when it can disregard the last instruction and get on with its life! This short command is one of the most important in the relationship between you and your hound. When used religiously it will build the trust in your hound that you will release it from an earlier command. Fail to do this and you will soon have a dog that creeps forward at the 'stay' or takes a few steps away when told to 'wait'.

'Get here' or 'come back'

The recall is vastly important and much more difficult to instill with a dog as fast as a lurcher than with a slow dog. Luckily, with Dylan, simple command and reward techniques (treats, pats on the head) soon had him trotting back to my 'Get here!' call. Disobedience must never see you chastising the dog when he eventually returns or the dog will reason that the returning, not the staying away, has offended you. Disastrous. Always greet the returning dog with affection, crouching to his face level. If you've bonded well, long before field training, the dog should recognise when he has pleased or annoyed you.
There are some very simple techniques to use with a puppy that starts to range away and not return to your call. They need to be used early and often, before the penny drops that actually, you're not fast enough to catch him! Both were effective with Dylan, who wanted to follow me everywhere. One is to disappear if he's ignoring you … duck behind a tree or hedge if possible … then call the pup. His discomfort when he can't see you will soon make him come looking for you. The second is to just crouch down and act as if you've found something interesting. A pups curiosity will normally bring it back in to investigate. Again, remember to crouch down at his return and make a fuss. If recall training is failing miserably you are going to face some difficult decisions. You can't take such a dog hunting, particularly amongst stock or near roads. In the UK, farmers still have the right to shoot on sight a dog which is worrying stock. Another reason why instant recall is so important to the dogs owner.

One of the keys to recall training is keeping the dogs attention. In a ground level world painted with new, fresh and exciting scents to follow any dog can be forgiven for being led by its olfactory senses. It will want to explore every nook and cranny, cross the fence, go through the gateway. Like a distracted child your pup will lose focus on everything but this new adventure. An important trait for the hunter is to share this excitement with the pup. Keep talking to it, so that it is forced to re-engage with you constantly and remember that you are there. *"What is it, boy!"* or *"What have you found?"*. If you know the dog is following rabbit sign, encourage it with talk and association. *"Where's the rabbits?"*. If you are inter-acting with the hound it is less likely to run off. If it tries to range away, call it back immediately firmly but in a friendly way. *"C'mon boy! Get here"*. Turn and walk the other way, don't chase after the dog … no matter how much that urge seizes you.

Quite often the returning pup gets reasonably close but won't come to you, sensing it has done wrong. It does no harm to re-enforce this slightly by walking away a bit further and ignoring the pup. Then turn and squat, calling the pup in vigorously and praise it when it arrives. Reward with a treat if you have one. You need the dog to know right behaviour from wrong.

If I'm making all this sound easy … it isn't! You need the patience of a saint when training recall. In some breeds (spaniels are typical) the prey drive is so strong that once their nose is down it's very difficult to regain their attention when they are young. If solid and dedicated training goes in during that first year, with any breed, your dog will mature with an understanding that being at its masters or mistresses side is a very rewarding place to be. If you don't put that training in, your dog might not even survive to maturity.

Now, this a very contentious subject but I have seen belligerent and un-biddable dogs transformed very quickly with careful use of electronic or buzzer collars and in my opinion that is far preferable to a dog being dumped into a rescue or re-homing sanctuary. Of course it's not an ideal choice. Nor should it be used as a 'shortcut' to normal training and bonding. The principle of so-called 'shock' training is that a small charge delivered to the dogs neck via the collar will scare it at a time when it's misbehaving … at a considerable distance. It will associate that misbehaviour with the shock, particularly after repetition. There is an inherent problem here though. Too many trainers use the system silently, with no voice command. Which is stupid. If you are trying to train a dog to associate misbehaviour with disapproval or reprimand, you need to vocalise the required behaviour … such as saying 'Get here!' if you expect the dog to come back to you. Perhaps 'No!' if it is chasing away.

During Dylans puppy training we hit a crisis period when he was about nine months old. In dog terms, teenage rebellion. He developed that dangerous trait of ignoring recall and sprinting off in a local park. A young lurcher can turn in speeds of up to 30mph so I had no chance of catching him. The first night this happened he leapt into a play area, fenced off from dogs, and terrified the toddlers merely due to his size (he wasn't aggressive but try explaining that to an angry parent!). The next night he disappeared totally. I searched the local estate, calling his name and feared I'd lost him. I found him on my doorstep, trembling. He would have had to cross three busy roads to get there. I was both relieved and horrified, to think that not only could he have been killed but could have caused a serious accident. I made a phone call to friend, a gun-dog trainer.

On the third night he entered the park fitted with an electronic collar. The first time I had ever had to use one in my life. I had tested it on myself first and found it no worse than one of those silly joke-shop handshake tricks. I kept him on the lead for a while then, in the middle of the park, let him off and threw a ball for him to retrieve. Which he did. A few times. Then I saw that wild glint in his eye and he turned to run off. I called him immediately … 'Get here!' Which checked him, as it had other nights. He turned, shot me a look of defiance and started to sprint. I shouted 'Noooo!' loudly and hit the button. I had already turned to walk away, so only heard a weak yelp (lurchers are notorious wimps). As I walked on, Dylan joined beside me, looking up at me for protection. We stayed in the park and I threw the ball some more. Twice more, the sprint for freedom. Twice more, I hit the button as I shouted 'Noooo!', walking away from the dog.

That third time, I hadn't used the shock button. I had used the buzzer. A little vibration. On the fourth time, when he ran and defied the 'get here!' command, I had it turned to shock again but didn't press. I just shouted 'Noooo!'. He checked his run and came back to walk alongside me. I never had to use that collar again. Ten years on, when I shout 'Noooo!' my dog knows it is in his best interest to comply. That was two hours with a training collar, well spent.

Lead Training

Personally, I've often found this the most harrowing and frustrating part of training a pup. Yet in a world of metalled roads, fast cars, free-ranging domestic cats and a host of canine temptation, the leash is an essential piece of equipment for the hunting-dog owner. This is definitely a 'must-do' as soon as the pup is inoculated and ready to meet the big wide world. In fact, it is the privilege of meeting the big wide world that should underpin lead training. No leash, no big wide world, no exercise. Your pup will be used to running around the yard or garden unchecked. It is used to being handled and fussed. You will, I hope, have placed a light collar around its neck so that it is used to it. If you didn't, go back to square one and start again. A pup used to a collar is less likely to resist the leash. If you have a garden, leash training should start there. Slipping it on and off, walking a few paces up and down until the pup is used to it.

So, out you go. The first thing to remember is that those first few trips out may be terrifying to a young dog. So for the hunting dog I would recommend that you get straight into a car and take it somewhere quiet, rural, with few distractions. Slip the lead on and let the pup get used to you and that damned umbilical cord which links it to you and it will (initially) hate. Just think about this for a moment .. and I witness this regularly in urban/suburban areas .. the pups first experience of a leash is to be led outdoors into a maelstrom of noise, movement, bustle and smell. Cars, buses, planes, motorbikes, humans rushing past, many stopping to stoop over it and (imagine this from the pups perspective) touching it, patting it. The dog is terrified and the only thing stopping it from fleeing to safety and security is the thing you just wrapped around its neck.

If you've got the dog used to taking short walks in a quiet environment on the lead, it will associate the lead with pleasure and so venturing into urban or suburban walking will be better received. Even rural training will meet with resistance from some pups, regardless of breed. The pup that plants its little arse down and won't budge is the classic rebel. If tempting it forward with treats and tit-bits doesn't work , pick it up and put it back in the car (or back indoors if you are training in the garden). Don't take any nonsense. The dog needs to associate the leash with privilege. Just as, when your dog is trained fully, it will associate release from the leash with freedom and trust. Before long, your dog will associate the rattle of the leash with exercise and it will be bouncing off the walls when you pick it up.

'HEEL' OR 'WAIT'

Training a dog to walk to heel is more challenging than it first sounds. Particularly a rangy dog like a sight-hound. The animals natural gait will be longer and faster than a humans. Therefore forcing it to stay at your knee is a big ask for the dog. Sure, you see collies and herding dogs trained to this level at obedience shows but it just isn't natural. Nor would you see a working shepherd ask his or dog to adopt such absurd behaviour. The rifle hunters dog simply needs the ability to be controlled closely and kept within a safe range of the hunter. This is for a number of reasons including, but not exclusively, safety (stopping the hound ranging into the guns line of fire). Other reasons include preventing flushing of quarry, maintaining control near livestock and keeping the dog within sight. The '*heel*' command is an invisible check-lead which when uttered should make the dog stop and drift back within the hunters close proximity. It shouldn't have to hug your knee and look dolefully up at you like a trick-dog. The acceptable 'heel' range for my dog is within three or four yards.

I think it goes without saying that if you haven't mastered a dogs recall, you will have little success with '*heel*' training. Heel training is easily introduced during puppy stages while walking and exercising, using a long lead. Let the dog range out, give the 'heel' command and gently pull the dog in towards you. The subtle difference between recall and heel is that when you ask a dog to heel-in you will usually be moving. As with all training, always praise the dog when it comes back in. Young pups appreciate a treat but 'treat' training needs to be gradually reduced as a dog gets older.

In practise, in the field, I actually use two commands according to situation. I use a firm *'wait'* when my dog drifts too far in front, which halts him until I can catch up with him. I use *'heel'* only when I want him right back near me. How far I let him range ahead depends entirely on circumstances. Simply traversing fields or tracks I often let him scout ahead if there are no hazards or livestock. If we are actually 'hunting', i.e. stalking quarry, I will insist he stays close.

It's probably worth mentioning here that Dylan has another word in his vocabulary that he understands succinctly. The word is *'Dangerous!'* and was trained in when he was a pup, on the lead, and we stopped at busy roads. He associates the word with traffic and if we are hiking (not necessarily hunting) and I see a metalled road or spot a moving vehicle on a trail, that word will check him and he will wait for me to slip the lead on. Always remember that your dog, with such low field of view, can't always see the hazards you can see.

'Drop'

There is a subtle difference between the 'stay' and the 'drop' command, even though both may result in the same posture (the dog laying prone). The 'drop' is taught to get a dog to lie swiftly, close to you. This can be for a variety of reasons. Approaching people, stock or quarry usually. For instance, I will drop Dylan when strangers or trespassers are approaching us (sometimes to reduce his threat and sometimes to accentuate it .. read on!). A large dog like a deerhound cross lurcher can worry some people, even though they are gentle-natured. If strangers are approaching, perhaps lost ramblers, they made need help so a controlling your dog is as courteous as dis-arming your rifle. A safe and natural thing to do. If, however, you find yourself subject to confrontation (as I have many times, from anti-hunting types) simply standing your dog may be enough to discourage any further argument! And is certainly better than arming you gun. Never, ever do that! If a farmer, farm-hand or their family approach me I always make a point of dropping the dog. Not only does it display courtesy but also complete control of the hound, which will always impress.

The 'drop' command is useful in many actual hunting scenarios. When you note a flock of wood-pigeon flighting in to roost, you will want to reduce your hounds profile. When you hear the cackle of a magpie or the croak of a crow, you need to hide the dog swiftly. You see a grey squirrel bounding towards you up a forest ride and need to conceal your dog. Whisper 'drop' and extend a hand, palm down, to hide your dog from the squirrel which will see anything higher than ground level.

'Go Fetch!'

Teaching a dog to search out and retrieve is relatively easy if initiated from puppy-hood. Throwing a rolled up sock a few yards and encouraging the pup to chase it is simple. That is its natural instinct. Persuading the pup to carry the sock back to you is a little more challenging, usually needing encouragement through a small reward. Get the pup used to the fact that until the sock is released into your hand without a tug-of-war, there will be no treat or pat or on the head. During these little games, which should be played for a short time only lest the pup loses interest, you will be using the 'go fetch' command. Gradually extend the distance and also vary the object being fetched. This is all easy stuff and lays the foundation for the more advanced skill you need in your future hunting companion.

Next, get the growing pup used to fetching objects that it hasn't seen thrown. Hidden treasure. Pups love this game and with Dylan I started it in the house. Simply 'stay' the dog and let it sniff the sock (or other toy). Wander off around the house, out of sight and tuck the sock under a bed or behind chair … somewhere the pup can reach. Return to the dog, rub your hands on its nose so that it gets the scent and send it off to 'go fetch' the object. This wonderfully simple hunting game will train your dog for much bigger challenges out in the field. As with all training exercises, little and often is the key to keeping the pup interested. As always, the dog needs to learn to return the toy to your hand and release it.

If the dog shows a tendency to 'possess' the toy, take it in your hand and use the other hand to gently prise open the pups teeth until it releases. Use a firm release command (I use 'dead!'). If a dog refuses to release, lightly covering its nostrils with your palm will make life uncomfortable enough to prompt a release. You want to reach a standard where the dog will either to pass live quarry to hand or release dead game at your feet. This will depend, of course, on your particular shooting discipline. For this reason you must never, ever allow a tug-of-war with the dog. The prize is yours, not the dogs. It needs to learn that.

Transferring the 'go fetch' discipline into the hunting field is a natural progression for most dogs. The only complication will be the dogs acceptance (or not) of either live or dead game. For this reason, most trainers will use dummies wrapped in rabbit fur or bird feathers to get the adolescent dog used to mouthing such an (initially) alien material. When it comes to actual retrieving, some dogs will love fur and hate feather (Dylan is like this, I'm afraid) or vice-versa. Some will at first baulk at live game and only fetch dead. Some pups will run a mile from a kicking rabbit or flapping bird. Others will pounce and finish the job.

Sending the dog to fetch needs some common-sense, of course. Be aware of hazards, livestock and traffic. Most dogs, when their nose is down and they're on the trail are oblivious to everything else except completing the retrieve.

'STAY'

This command really is the toughest one, in my humble opinion. The older the pup gets and the more you bond with it, particularly out in the hunting field, the more reluctant your pup will be to let you out of its sight. Yet, ultimately, that's what's you are about to train your pup to do .. and it takes a lot of patience.

So first, I can hear you ask 'Why is it important to train a hunting dog to *stay*?' It's a good point and I know very few hunters who instil this discipline into their hound. Yet for me, an air rifle hunter, it is a vital command for a number of reasons. If I'm stalking hedgerows and margins after rabbits, I need to be able to creep carefully around gateways and openings to check for quarry browsing on the other side, out of view. I always *stay* Dylan, my lurcher, and lay him on the ground while I check for quarry. If the coast is clear, I call him in to me with a flick of the finger or (if he can see me) a pat on the thigh. I may be stalking wood-pigeon under the tree canopy. I will be trying carefully not to throw a shadow across the woodland floor but I can't expect my dog to consider this. So he may have to wait lying under cover until I've finished my stalk. On occasions, I have to challenge trespassers (usually lost ramblers). He is a big dog! I will usually '*stay*' him in sight nearby, shoulder the rifle on its sling and go to talk to them. There are numerous reasons for training in this level of discipline and one of them is .. if you can, why wouldn't you?

The '*stay*' command is the proverbial elephant for consumption. How do you eat an elephant? In small bite sized chunks, of course. You will start by laying your little pup in the garden, on the grass, saying '*stay*' and walking away half a dozen steps. It will immediately get up and follow you. After ten minutes of this, you will want to scream with frustration. And this is just day one. Remember my earlier chapter 'Think Like A Dog'? Well, your pup is feeling confused too so go easy on it.

You should by now have already taught the sit or lie down commands, and the recall. Lay the pup, say '*Stay!*' firmly, hold out your hand, palm facing the pup and slowly back away, palm still up. Keep repeating the *stay* command. Just take a few steps. If the pup moves just say 'No!', take it back and lay it again. Repeat this, always facing the dog, but watch for the moment it is about to follow and move towards the dog instead and with palm up, repeat '*Stay!*'. If the dog stays down, reward it with a treat. If it moves, don't. Until the pup associates just lying there with reward, keep the distance between you and the dog minimal. Only practice for ten minutes at a time or the pup will get bored and you will get frustrated. Over a period of weeks, you will gradually extend the distance that you back away. You will constantly correct the dog for 'creeping forwards' and the dog must learn to trust that it will be released with a 'get here' or your normal recall command. From here you need to progress to walking away with your back to the dog. For the pup, this is another quantum leap in trust so at first you will constantly check over your shoulder repeating the *stay* command. When you can sit fifty yards from your dog for five minutes and it doesn't budge, you've cracked it. Nearly!

Next you are going to *stay* your dog and move out of sight for a short time. This is the ultimate test of trust between dog and hunter. Your hound is definitely on that invisible leash and if you are worried about the pup, your pup is sure as hell worried what you're up to! First of all, *stay* your dog close to the ideal situation to carry out such an exercise. A gate in a walled meadow is ideal, or a outside a barn in the farmyard. Even if your dog is resolute on the *stay* in the open, with you in sight, this exercise will disturb it, so make sure that you won't get any distractions. *Stay* the dog, back away slowly repeating the *stay* command and edge out of sight for a few seconds. Don't overdo it. Step back into sight. If your pup stayed firm, make a big fuss and reward it. If it crept forward, gently take it back, re-assure the pup and try again. Don't spend long on each training session. As with all training, you should teach for short bursts over a number of weeks. The first task is get the dog staying firm when you are out of sight for just a short time. When that is achieved, gradually extend the time you remain out of sight. Remember, though, that you're not out set a world record. Personally, my dog is of far more value to me than any gun .. and I never let any gun out of my sight! As described above, there are a few occasions when you will want to proceed on a stalk or hunting sortie for moments without your dog disturbing your hunt. I honestly can't think of a time when I have required Dylan to *stay*, out of my sight-line, for more than a few minutes. That's all you need from your hound. Three minutes patience.

Once again the release command is so, so important in this exercise. I always recall Dylan from the '*stay*' from where I am at the time. Once trained, you don't need to go back for the dog. Simply summon it with a call or a low whistle. In saying this, exercise caution and common sense. Your dog will be keen to rejoin you so if you've crossed a dyke or barbed-wire fence, don't recall it blind or you will put it at risk. Go back to the safe side or go right back to your dog.

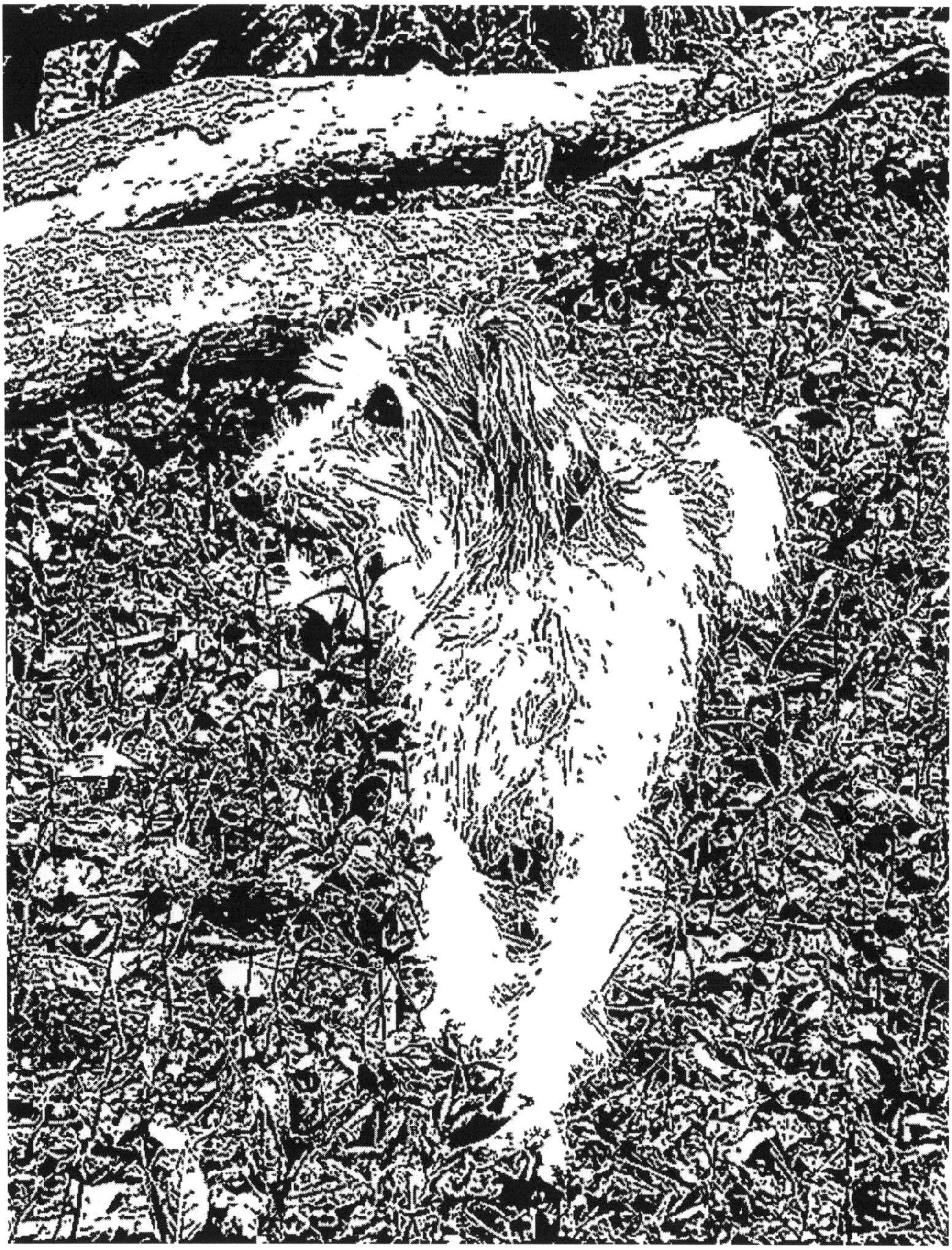

'LEAVE!'

Before the liberty of free-ranging is allowed, you have one vital training task to test first. Stock training. This should have started way back at a few months old, on the lead. It should be re-affirmed now around the farm and fields before trusting a dog off the lead. An unsteady dog will very soon lose you your shooting permission so this is one of the most important disciplines that you will instil in your shooting companion. The *'Leave!'* command. Like many advanced training commands, this is taught through association.

You bought a hunting breed pup for good reason. It is genetically programmed to seek out, flush, mark or chase quarry. Yet like the hunter themselves, there will be good reason too to exercise restraint. The rifle hunter can't point a rifle at everything that steps within range. It may be the wrong season for buck or doe, for species even. The shot may be unsafe or unethical. You may be using the wrong calibre for that quarry. You may have simply been asked by the land-owner to conserve that species. There will be many occasions in a shooters lifetime when they have to lower the barrel and accept .. not now! Perhaps another day? That same discipline needs to be trained into the hunters dog. Checking the natural urge to hunt, chase and particularly (as it is deeply ingrained in some breeds) not to 'worry' livestock. The almost cartoon-like hatred exhibited by many dogs towards cats is not unique to any breed, I know. The problem you have with a lurcher (or any other sight-hound) is their actual ability to connect with the enemy if you don't have your wits about you! They are fast enough to. Dylan is no different, so vigilance is imperative near cats.

'Over 'and 'Jump'

The hunters dog is absolutely useless if it can't negotiate the many barriers and hurdles it may encounter in the field. That doesn't necessarily mean, however, that it has to jump everything. There used to be, in opinion, an unhealthy competitiveness in lurcher circles about high your dog could jump. I've never been interested in this. It resulted in too many lame or crippled animals. My own lurcher can leap a five bar gate comfortably but I rarely ask him to. Landing on frost-hardened mud or slippery grass beyond a gate is a recipe for serious injury. No .. I prefer my dog to use his intelligence and seek a sensible way around any barrier. This might mean ranging along a fence or hedgerow to find a way through. He's had enough stitches during his life to know now how to slide under a barbed wire strand carefully, not hastily.

Teaching jumping is easy and a pup will find it fun if you start with low barriers and gradually increase the height. A barrier at the garden door is perfect because the pup will want follow you when you step over. Always use the 'Jump' command just before it leaps and it will soon become familiar. Just keeping building the height by a few inches at a time. Praise the dog heartily when it clears the jump. Outdoors, encourage the pup over low hurdles like fallen tree stumps. Don't neglect ditches, dykes and drains either. Spot opportunities to challenge the pups athleticism and jumping to command will become second nature.

Importantly, here, also train your dog not to take potentially harmful or suicidal action to follow you. If you come to a barrier obviously hazardous to the dog, help it seek a way through elsewhere. Under wire, through a gap in a hedge, perhaps through a drainage tunnel. Make the dog 'stay' on the other side then find your route over and recall the dog. It is for exactly this reason that I use the 'Over' command in these situations so that dog knows it means 'find your way through' not 'Jump'. It encourages the dog to use its brain not its athletic instinct.

THE BRIDGE ENCOUNTER

I had been granted access to some new shooting permission, part of which bordered a tributary cut of the River Wensum near Norwich. I was keen to explore an island in the middle of the cut which looked like a perfect spot for pigeon roost-shooting. Lots of ivy-strangled alder trees. I also knew the spot was noted for herons and otters so on the first visit, I loaded my bag with some photographic gear too. Against my better judgement, I took Dylan along for this first serious visit, having only previously viewed it from the motor. It was a bitterly cold foggy February afternoon, perfect for roost shooting. The cut was about eight yards wide and the only way over to the island was a wide beam of wood, some two feet wide. There was nothing to hold on to so it would be just a cautious stroll across. I laid Dylan on the turf of the river bank and told him to stay, intending to call him across once I'd made the other side. What happened next lasted just three or four seconds but I can still see it all in slow-motion as I did at the time! I took about three confident strides onto the bridge and my lead foot slid away. The surface was covered with a treacherous layer of mould, as slippery as ice. I shouted "Hell!" yet, somehow, I managed to regain my balance and save the £2000 worth of camera kit in the bag and the £1200 rifle combo slung over my shoulder from a drenching. Out of the corner of my eye I saw the dog launch himself onto the bridge, probably concerned for me. I screamed "Nooo!" but it was too late. I braced my legs for the impact. Dylan hit a patch of slime and skidded into my legs, bouncing off into the four foot deep dyke, leaving me tottering. Again I held my balance, took a deep breath and paced carefully onto the island, throwing down all my gear. I ran to the bank and Dylan was paddling and desperately trying to get a purchase on the soft muddy bank but kept slipping back and going under. He was panicking now in the fast flowing and freezing water but I managed to call him up the bank again and he got high enough for me to grab his collar. His weight nearly pulled me back in with him but I snatched at an alder sapling with my other hand and pulled him up to safety. After an initial barrage of expletives which questioned his intelligence and whether he had a known father, I stood looking at the shivering hound. Anyone who has ever seen a wet lurcher will know what I mean. They look pathetic. Priority now was to get the traumatised dog back into warmth. The worst part, of course, was that we were now on the island which meant we had yet to go back! I stood him at the end of the plank and asked him to go 'over'. Not surprisingly, he wouldn't set a paw on the bridge. I tied him to a tree so he couldn't follow me, the dis-armed rifle next to him, then crossed the bridge gingerly carrying just bag. When that was over at least I knew the camera and lenses were safe. Yeah, I'm insured but I wasn't sure how a loss-adjustor would view my claim form ('I was crossing a narrow, slippery plank over a river in the middle of winter and my dog barged me into the water')? I edged back and untied the dog and told him 'Over!' He set off slowly and I followed behind to make sure he didn't change his mind. He paused and made to turn twice but I firmly kept up the 'Over!' He leapt the last few feet. On the other side I again tied him up and went back for the rifle. Dylan was by now shivering, a mixture of both cold and shock, so it was straight home into the warm and a good towel down. After a warm meal, he soon recovered and we've been over that bridge many times since in drier, safer conditions.

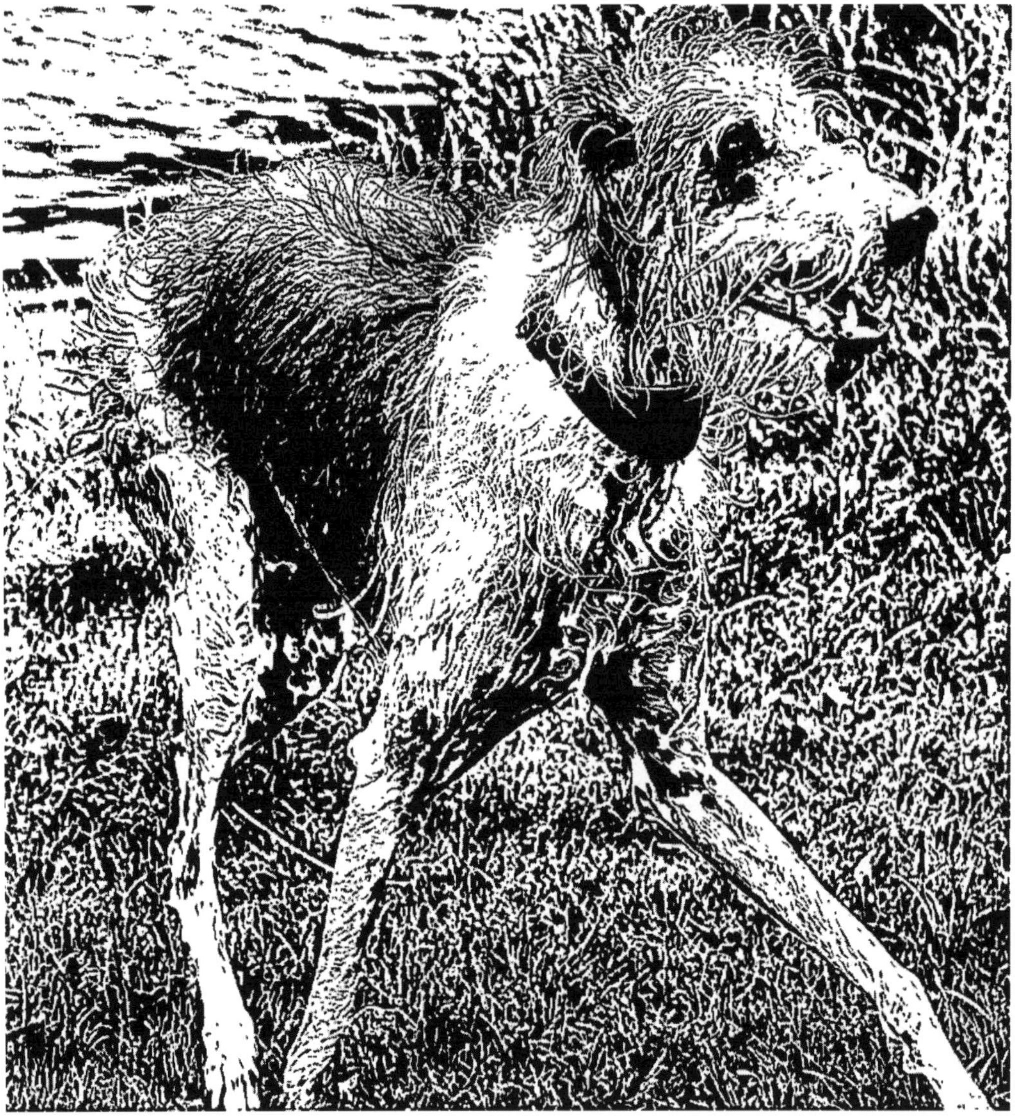

'LOOK ABOUT'

Whenever I want my lurcher to actively search about and flush quarry, this is the command I use. Though there are few occasions when a rifle hunter needs the dog to do this, it is a useful instruction. The shot-gunner, of course, needs this all the time but both small bore rifle shooters and air-gunners like me can't (as in shouldn't) be firing at moving quarry. Even pests like fox, rat, coyote, squirrel, crow, pigeon and rabbit deserve the respect of a clean despatch, which means shooting the creature when it is stationary so that the hunter can zero in on the kill-zone ... not just injure the creature.

Remember that (as mentioned elsewhere) your focal range is some three or four feet above that of your hound. You will see things ahead while hunting that the dog can't. It's in these situations that I often use the 'look about' command. Dylan may be following squirrel scent, nose down. I spot the squirrel on the ground twenty yards ahead, perhaps shielded from the dogs view by a screen of briar or fern. This command will tell the dog that that I've seen the quarry. In many cases I will shoot without alerting the dog. If the quarry is on the move or goes into cover and I alert the dog, he will help flush the squirrel and push it into the tree-line. Nine times out of ten, a squirrel pushed to flight by a dog will scamper up the nearest tree trunk and cling to the bark on the blind side of any alien movement, like a lizard hugging a hot wall. My 'look about' command will send the dog moving around the tree, forcing the squirrel to shuffle around to my side. A sitting duck. The threat is the dog, which is pursuing it. It will forget I'm there, with a gun aimed at it.

This is a useful command on rabbits too, just to get the dog alert to the fact that you've seen them ahead and to stop it ranging out and disturbing them. I know, from watching my hound, that he gets very frustrated knowing that I've seen quarry (especially when I raise the rifle to something he can't also see). Keeping him alert but his enthusiasm in check is therefore important until I can release to retrieve.

'CATCH!'

This is a natural progression from the 'look about' command and is the command I use to ask my dog to actually chase, find and kill. With due regard to current (ridiculous) laws surrounding hunting, the use of dogs and legal quarry this is a command sometimes required to ensure humane dispatch of winged or injured quarry. Nothing chases down 'pricked' quarry faster than a hunting hound. A human blundering across scrub, plough or grassland seeking to put an injured creature out of its misery is a pathetic sight. I know .. I have been that sad specimen. I'm long enough in the tooth and broad enough in the shoulder to admit that I sometimes get it all wrong and so sending my dog out to put right my mistake and ensure the swift dispatch of injured quarry is more important to me than adherence to idiot laws underwritten by folk with no understanding of the countryside and its natural order.

Thus, this command has been understood by my dog, over a period of time to mean 'licensed to kill' and has prevented suffering to all manner of creatures. Any injured animal or bird will look for sanctuary immediately. Their first natural instinct is to hide from further danger. The dogs nose and hearing will soon find the poor animal and allow you to finish what you started. In terms of rifle work, with a single shot opportunity which can go wrong even if expertly undertaken (the quarry steps forward as you shoot, flies upwards, floats downwards, stands, sits .. so much can happen in that split second that the trigger is tickled), the availability of a trained dog is crucial.

The dog isn't always given the 'catch' command due to creatures that I have shot poorly either (I don't often get it so wrong that I need to send in the dog!). Myxied rabbits, injured birds, snared vermin. All can be dealt with in seconds by a large, fast dog such as a lurcher.

INTRODUCING THE PUP TO HUNTING

When you have a dog that sits, recalls confidently and stays close to you and obeys the *'leave!'* command then you have a dog ready to introduce to rifle hunting. It will need to be mature enough physically to negotiate barriers and hedges and spend hours out in the field with you in all manner of weather conditions. By all means take a younger pup out and about on a lead while shooting, to let it learn, but I wouldn't advocate letting a dog free-range before nine months to a year old.

Like the hunter, the dog will learn fastest in the field, often through its own mistakes, therefore it needs the maturity to distinguish between failure and success. It needs the maturity to understand when restraint (obeying your command) is preferential to disobedience. That is hard enough for the mature dog to accept. The young pup has no chance of comprehending this. This isn't just about mental maturity either. It also about physiological maturity. Stamina, strength, endurance. Bones rigid enough to run and jump without injury. Muscles and tendons developed to sustain a day in the field. A coat and skin tolerant of cold, wind, rain or worse. Pads toughened enough to cross plough, flint and rock.

The young dog being introduced to the field is no different to the child being blooded for the first time. There is an in-bred excitement and a genetic desire to 'kill' without yet understanding the responsibility attached to the decision to end another creatures life. In the pup, this is more natural than in a child but the outcome of that first association with death can often be similar. I can still remember the elation at that first starling (back then, they were still legal quarry) with an air rifle yet the feeling of guilt when I picked it up and handled it. So vibrant in the scope, so limp and pathetic in my hands. With the pup, this is completely different. They can't exhibit emotion. It is more likely to be fear that it associates with it's first kill, depending on how the kill happened and the quarry involved. Hence the warning about maturity. A six month old lurcher, for instance, that collects an injured (not cleanly killed) rabbit or grey squirrel is likely to encounter trouble. The rabbit, due to its weight, will match the pup and can kick or struggle. The squirrel (rats are the same) can clamp to a pups snout viciously and those teeth (in jaws designed to crack cob nuts) can cause a lot of damage. Result? A quarry-shy pup. Disaster. Now, perhaps, you will appreciate the importance of maturity and that precious *'Leave!'* command?

Herein, though, lies a tough contradiction. You don't want a rifle trained dog to chase and kill on instinct. You are breaking them of their ingrained kill instinct, through your training. Yet you want them to associate with quarry. Very often (and this certainly happened with Dylan) when led to a freshly shot but very dead rabbit the pup will view it with trepidation and fear. I can't explain this other that to suggest that the pup is thinking *'Jeez .. Something killed it! It wasn't me? So am I in danger?'*. With Dylan this was quickly overcome. I just picked up fresh rabbits and animated them. The same with squirrels. Just wave them about. Let the blood scent spread. Then throw them a few feet away. The pups predator instinct will kick in and it will react by pouncing on the dead quarry. Simple.

There are a number of things to consider when taking a dog into the hunting field. Some are obvious (like the need for water, a blanket and a first aid kit in the motor). Some are far less obvious and only learnt through experience (or advice like this). For most hunting hounds the first thing they will do, once they realise that this is a 'hunt', will be to defecate on leaving a car or trailer. This is a primal instinct and can be seen in virtually all canine species. Wolves, foxes, coyotes, Cape hunting dogs, jackals .. they all do this. The main reason seems to be a need to 'lighten the load' before chasing but who really knows? Certainly, racing greyhounds do this before entering the traps .. which lends some credence to the theory. Now this habit might seem innocuous to you but unless you've planned your trail carefully, this scent travelling down-wind to your quarry source is going to be the biggest advert to predation that you can send! Think carefully about where you are going to disembark your dog before a hunt.

Think about this trait, too? Dogs are prone to rolling in all manner of (to us) disgusting substances. Should you reprimand or encourage this obnoxious behaviour? If I explain why they do it, I can leave the answer to you. As in the paragraph above, this is a primal behaviour passed down through all canines hunting genes. The dog is disguising its own strong musk with another rank or foetid scent which will be familiar to, but not threatening to, the dogs prey. In order to get in closer to its quarry before launching an attack. If your dog is a 'house dog' .. and I would advocate that the rifle hunters dog should be .. then it's not advisable to let your dog follow its natural urge if you want to keep the rest of the household happy! My lurcher is very partial to either rotting rabbit remains or, strangely, decomposing gulls washed up on the tide-line. Quite how he associates with hunting gulls is beyond me!

Once you get the young dog into the field and start working it to live quarry, quarry association will come naturally and only through following you about and learning. The trick is to just hunt as though you don't have a dog with you for the first few months. Every species you shoot will educate the dog. Let it sniff, mouth, retrieve, chase down 'runners'. The dog can only learn by association. It will quickly learn to associate patterns, therefore what quarry is present. The chatter or the rustle of the grey squirrel in the tree-tops, its scent on the floor, tree trunks and natural feeding tables, the scratching of tiny claws on bark. The cackle or the chuckle of magpies. The scream of the jay. The murmur of the wood-pigeon and its clatter into the branches above. The drumming of the rabbits hind leg. The lingering scent of rabbit urine, virtually undetectable to you but over-powering to your hound. Depending on your personal shooting discipline, these patterns will vary. The musk or the scats of the red fox will be easily marked by your dog. The scent of pheasant or partridge. The sounds too .. the *'chack'* of the latter and the crowing of the former. Dogs learn very fast and put all these clues into the memory bank. The bark of the roe or muntjac. The scent of the fresh deer currants. The sniff at the clump of hair on the barbed wire fence.

All of this formative education (while following you around) soon changes to scenting, pointing and marking ahead of you. The dog hunts, when you wish it to, and you follow ... taking advantage of your loyal hounds far superior senses. Every time the dog indicates a quarry type, you will be wise to both praise it and name it. This is the prequel to hunting to command. If your dog sniffs deer currants, pat it and say 'Deer!'. If its hare, say hare. Rabbit, squirrel, pheasant, whatever. When the dog realises that you shoot magpies and you both hear a magpies chatter, say 'Magpie!'. Dogs have a magnificent capacity for vocabulary. I expand on both aspects, association and vocabulary, in other chapters.

Once you've taught your dog to associate a word (name) with quarry, you can start directing the dog to hunt to command. By that I mean to ignore other prey and concentrate on one. If you watch your hound carefully, you will soon come to recognise that it marks various quarry types in a slightly different way. These will be small nuances but they are there, trust me. For instance, Dylan marks all close game with a lift of the left paw but a low lift tells me it's quarry he's forbidden, like pheasant or partridge. A high lift tells me it is our shooting quarry. Squirrel or rabbit. If he's looking upward, he is marking grey squirrels. If he is pointing, nose straight and back rigid, it's rabbits. If he has sensed large game his demeanour is different. He still hangs that paw but if it's fox his hackles go up (the same for cats). If it's badger he scents, his ears pin back and his tail goes between his legs. Dylan has never met a badger face to face but clearly understands their ferocity. The whole point of training to hunt to command is to avoid wasted time and hone in on the task at hand. Thus, when I get a call from a landowner complaining at the increase in squirrel activity I can unload my lurcher from the tailgate of my motor and just say 'Squirrel!'. He'll be off in front, nose to the ground seeking squirrel sign.

A huge point to make about introducing the pup to the hunting game is that it should happen slowly, patiently and without long days in the field. When disaster strikes, cut the hunting and restore the pups confidence with 'play'. Never, ever chastise a hunting apprentice (this applies to kids, too) for failure. Shrug your shoulders, comfort the pup and move on. Just like us as shooters, your dog will learn more from the near misses than the hits. Respect that.

Your Dogs Vocabulary

Trust me when I say that dogs can talk. No .. let me explain that! Dogs can understand human talk. One of the key principles within this book is the importance of associative training. There is no clearer example of this than watching an experienced old hunting dog react to a few words that accidentally slip off the tongue in an idle conversation between two humans. With my old lurcher, if someone simply mentions the word 'shooting' he will start bouncing off the walls. Though there are many other words that catch his attention .. words not necessarily associated with instruction or command. Most dogs soon recognise the words 'walk', 'lead' or 'dinner'.

I described in an earlier chapter (Introducing To Hunting) how over a period of time you can teach your hound to hunt specific species to command. Dylan can understand the words 'rabbit', 'hare' and 'squirrel'. And through long association of bird and animal sounds in the hunting field he can differentiate between those which we shoot and those we don't. He will ignore the crow of the pheasant, the chuck of the partridge or the bark of the muntjac deer. Yet he comes alert at the sound of the jays screech, the magpies chatter, the crows harsh croak or the hiss of an angry squirrel and will look towards me to check my gun is raised.

There may be reasons to 'teach' further words to your dog. I taught 'Dangerous!' to make my pup traffic-conscious but on reflection it could just have easily been 'Car!'. It happened after having to haul the pup by his lead from the road, several times, when he simply didn't associate an oncoming vehicle with danger, didn't stop and just stepped out.

Silent Commands

Whether in the woods and fields, around the farmyard, along the hedgerow, bird and beast have mastery over the hunter. Their senses .. sight, sound, scent and that acute sixth sense which detects malice .. give them an advantage which makes the whole exercise of hunting and vermin control a noble cause. In setting out to train my lurcher to work alongside me in the field, I had a vision of the perfect hound. A 'ninja' hound. One that would steal along at my side like those legendary old poachers dogs. A hound that would lie down to a hand signal, return to heel at a flick of the finger, push on into cover with a click of the tongue, recall from the 'stay' to a low whistle, go left or right ahead of me with a silent command. A tall order, particularly from a hunter who had never attempted such a high level of training before. Yet, as it says in the great Tao Te Ching, "In Nature, nothing is hurried yet everything is achieved".

Over the first few years I also accompanied some commands with a flick of the finger, a click of the tongue or a hand signal until eventually, I could get Dylan to work to these alone. Hence we can now work together in almost total silence in wood or field. A raised hand, palm down, means 'stay' and he will lie down. A pat on my thigh is his release signal and he will get up and follow me. A flick of the finger means 'heel in' and he will return close to me. A double click of the tongue means 'look about!', bringing him alert. Again, by association, Dylan learnt basic directional hand signals. When the pup ranges to your left, wave your hand that way and vice versa for the right. Soon the dog will understand. When we come to a crossroad on a woodland ride, Dylan will stop and look to me and I can send him in the direction I want him to take without uttering a word.

The rifle hunter wants to work at all times in relative silence so I have never used a dog-whistle during training. They are just too disruptive. The only exception I make is when we lose sight of each other and I have to give the dog a sound to focus on to find me, which is then just a bird-like whistle using my mouth.

Health & Welfare

General maintenance is wise to keep your dog in tip-top condition. Keeping claws trimmed and also grooming the coat (a nightmare with Dylan, who has more dreadlocks than Bob Marley). Checking the coat for fleas and ticks after every outing (and removing them). Inspecting toes and pads for cuts, grazes, thorns, burrs or any alien items. The dog will generally self-cleanse after work but burrs are a perfect example of why you should intervene first. Burrs, pulled out by a dogs teeth, break up into tiny barbs which stick to the dogs tongue and end up swallowed. These barbs (when caught in the dogs throat) cause coughing, gagging, soreness, lack of appetite and general malaise. Get them out before the dog tries to!

First aid is a whole other subject where I'm not prepared to go too deeply. I'm simply not a fan of the DIY veterinary mentality. Hunting dogs get ripped and torn occasionally. A wise hunter, watching his or her dog carefully and treating it with respect, will minimise injury through careful control of the dog (in fact, the whole point of this book). When disaster strikes, however, my advice will always be (with due regard to emergency action such as a tourniquet or similar) get your dog to a vet! Forget the cost.

Permission and Stitches

When Dylan was about a year old I was given permission to shoot on a local farm. The farm was a mixture of arable, beef and a few sheep so, with plenty of pasture and stock, would be an ideal finishing school for the rapidly developing pup. I wouldn't normally broach the subject of bringing a dog onto a new farm until I'd gained the farmers complete trust but this was the perfect landscape so I posed the question. The young farmer told me to bring the pup on my walk of the boundaries and he'd see how he behaved. When I arrived, I was confident enough in my training to let him free-run but just to make sure he didn't let me down I slipped him on a lead before he jumped from the back of the motor, bouncing with the eternal optimism of youth. The first thing he did as the farmer looked on was evacuate his bowels. I drew a bag from my pocket and cleared up, the farmer showing me to a nearby bin. His old cattle herder, a cross-collie bitch, came to meet us and I slipped Dylan so that the pair could chase about and get familiar with each other. The farmer and his wife, who came out to see us, both loved the lurcher. We set off around the boundary of the farm so that the farmer could show the extent of his land and ensure I didn't upset any of his neighbours by trespassing. I had put Dylan back on the lead but the farmer said "Let him run, he'll be ok!" Half way round, the pup started to show an unhealthy interest in the cattle, not helped by the old collie running in to nip at their heels. I called him back with a firm "Leave!" and he scuttled back to my side. "Lord! He's a good 'un!" commented the farmer who then recalled his own dog. It was all going well until the collie spotted a browsing rabbit just inside a spinney on the opposite side of a barbed wire fence. The old bitch crept up on her belly until just under the slack, rusty wire. Dylan stood watching, head tilting from side to side. The collie, once under the wire, launched its chase with no prospect of success. Dylan, however, had decided that this was a game he wanted to be part of and set off like a missile before I could stop him. His youthful exuberance had calculated 'collie, chase, rabbit' but had forgotten the intermediate component 'barbed wire'. I grimaced as he hit the wire and rolled through with a squeal like a stuck pig. The collie returned to the farmer and I then had cajole the injured pup back under the wire, which I held up. Once bitten, twice shy ... he refused to come back and I had suffer the ignominy of climbing through, lifting him and passing him over to the farmer. We inspected Dylan and found just a half inch slash on the skin under his rib-cage. We carried on with the walk, the pup now somewhat subdued. Back at the car, the farmer confirmed the permission, which pleased me immensely. I told the pup to jump into the tailgate so that I could check his wound. The gash was now nearly three inches long and bleeding profusely. The farmer looked at me quizzically? I explained that a lurcher's skin tears like wet paper. Particularly at 'stress points' like the heaving rib-cage after a fast run. I had my permission. An hour later I also had a £100 vets bill to pay!

AN UNEXPECTED RABBIT

To my wife, Cheryl, our lurcher is perhaps a little more than the hunters companion. We've never had children as a couple so Dylan has always been treated as 'her boy'. Cheryl doesn't hunt, nor have any desire to, yet she has no objection to both 'her boys' hunting. There has always been this unwritten rule, however, that we leave the more gory aspects of dealing with quarry in the field if you get my drift. What happens in the field, stays in the field. My wife is happy to eat the meat harvested on our hunts but rarely sees it still dressed in fur or feather. One memorable moment in Dylan's puppy-hood came at a time when I was getting quite frustrated at his ability to snatch up rabbits of his volition. I was trying to encourage him to run and catch when not under the restrictions of the rifle. A tall ask (it's a wonder the poor lurcher didn't end up schizophrenic).
One day we were walking along a stretch of the Marriott Way near our home. This is a disused railway embankment now put to public use for walkers and cyclists as a long-distance byway between Aylsham and Norwich. It was a quiet, early Saturday morning on the path and we were letting the pup free-run. He had lagged behind a bit as we approached the car park at the end of the walk and I hadn't realised something had caught his attention. There were two little old ladies sauntering towards us with a rug-rat on a lead. As they neared us they were looking past us curiously. My wife and I spun round and there was Dylan about thirty yards back, bounding

towards us up the track, ragging a full grown buck rabbit! It must have been a third of his size so he wasn't finding his first live dispatch too easy! I managed to stop Cheryl from shouting any chastisement and met his retrieve. To his credit, by the time he got to me the rabbit was still and the pup was still shaking it, looking very pleased with himself. I then had a short battle with the youngster to get him to release his new trophy and slip a lead on him. With my back to the audience I stuffed the rabbit inside my coat and it started to kick. It was still alive! I walked back past the two confused ladies and a very embarrassed wife. "Beautiful morning, ladies!" I offered as we passed, hugging the struggling rabbit to my chest and we headed for the car. I drew out the coney and quickly necked it. Inside the car we burst into fits of laughter and next day had our first rabbit casserole provided by the young lurcher. Yet this had been another reason why the treasured 'leave!' command was ingrained early. That meant that we could enjoy our regular weekend rambles without having to hide a host of plundered game-birds or poached coneys! The pup soon learned to distinguish between 'work' and 'leisure'.

THE LATER YEARS

I mentioned in another chapter the danger in buying an allegedly 'trained' dog from a seller. You can see from all of the previous chapters that the hunter has to put heart and soul into bonding with a hound at this level. You simply don't sell a dog trained to this standard. You retire them when the time is right, hopefully bringing a pup along behind them in the field for the final year or two. An older dog can teach much to a younger one.

There will always be a difference in opinion on the wisdom of keeping on a dog that is past its prime and can contribute little more to the hunting game. My opinion is simple. The dog has bonded with me, worked its heart out for me, given me a lifetime of companionship and pleasure. So I owe the dog a comfortable retirement and any veterinary care it needs.

My current companion, Dylan, is approaching eleven as I write this. He is still fairly fit and lean though his eyes and hearing (like my own) are not what they were. Bringing in an apprentice is tempting but it is so hard to judge exactly when. We have such a unique bond, I may well grant him the respect of my sole attention and decline the opportunity to use him as a 'sensei'. For I know that a pup will steal my remaining time with him and he deserves better than that. We'll see.

THE PAPARAZZI POOCH

As Dylan's profile developed alongside mine in a variety of country-sports and shooting magazines I was regularly asked who followed me to take the photographs? Some of the more high-brow publications employ staff photographers and send them out to get commissioned pictures. I wouldn't ever entertain this as to my mind, two's company and three's a crowd. The 'two' being Dylan and I. It's for the same reason I refuse to do video-shoots. You can't hunt with a camera team following you. Not in my speciality, airgun hunting. For a while I flippantly commented in a couple of responses that I had trained Dylan to take photographs of me. It took me a while to realise that some people actually believed that! The penny didn't drop with me until I started to get replies such as "Wow! What a clever dog! But what about when you're both in the picture?" Unbelievable. After which, I started to feel guilty and explained that I make extensive use of radio-controlled remote shutter release. It was fun while it lasted but I had this over-riding vision of my dog being stolen by some unscrupulous 'paparazzi' photographer to wander into some superstars illicit poolside sexual liaison to get a scoop, tail wagging .. and failing! It's official, folks. Dylan does not take photographs. Sorry!

THE LAST WORD – FROM DYLAN

It's been an interesting journey, these past ten years. He's not a bad sort. I get to sleep in his house, I'm well fed and I get to walk out every day. In spring and summer we are often abroad with that confounded gun of his, but he seems to get pleasure from it. Personally, I would rather chase things but we came to an agreement when I was a pup that there were some occasions when I can chase but mostly I must stop still and give him the chance to shoot. Of course, over the years, I've developed a knack for forgetting to tell him that there is a coney squatting close by and occasionally sneak a dash at it. If I grab it, I get cussed no end. He has this swear word 'Bruised!' and shouts 'Leave it!' or 'Dead'. Which is daft, cos' I know it's dead. I've just killed it. Funny thing is, I always get to eat my own catches? We both like getting after the squirrels. I just wish he was a bit more alert? He never sees 'em until the last minute. Of course, he thinks he's a great shot. If only he knew how many of the little beggars I've had to give quick squeeze to satisfy his ego! When I bring them back to him he whispers 'Dead!' which is quite amusing. So I drop 'em at his feet and he's happy. Of course, they usually they are, but sometimes I wish I could say .. 'That one wasn't, Guv. Not until I nailed it!' Mind you, I could have a worse life. He's never sent me over a wire or gate in the pitch black just to get a coney. He's got a bit of sense about him. Never shouts at me either. Just a flick of the finger or a whisper. I wish he'd take me lamping more often, not that he lets me run the rabbits. Selfish beggar wants to shoot 'em with his light. Personally, I reckon he's scared of the dark! Oh .. and them big flashy birds all over the place? He won't let me nick one! Sometimes I look at him and say 'Go on, Guv'nor .. just one .. please?'

Postscript

I truly hope you've enjoyed the narrative above and found it useful. A short book, for sure ... but that really is because there is no black art in training a dog to the hunting rifle if you pick the right breed for the task and ignore the peer pressure often associated with shooting fraternity snobbery. A dog is not a 'marque' like a brand of rifle or shotgun or car. A dog shouldn't be paraded like a trophy-wife, nor should it be traded in or out of your life to suit your whim. The true shooter, the accomplished hunter, the real countryman or woman, will take a pup and mould it into the mature hound that will work for its master or mistress to its life's end.

This book is a tribute to such a hound. When Dylan leaves me to return into the Tao and hunt with the spirits of his myriad ancestors, perhaps to sit under a full moon and howl with the wolves, I will be heartbroken for a while. Then I will turn to the next pup, which will hopefully once again pick me, and we will work together to try to attain the standard that Dylan and I have reached together.

But then, who knows ... he may survive me? If you hear an old lurcher howling at the full moon under a wide Norfolk sky in the next few years, you will know whose it was. He will be checking that his old master is happy in his new wolf-pack.

About The Author

Ian Barnett is a freelance country-sports and hunting journalist based in Norfolk, England. Ian has hunted with airguns and lurchers since his teens and writes regularly for the airgun press about hunting fieldcraft. He is also a keen wildlife and landscape photographer. Many of Ians images can be seen on his Wildscribbler website (www.wildscribbler.co.uk). Ian also writes a regular blog on the website. Ians articles feature regularly in Airgun Shooter magazine and The Countrymans Weekly.

As well as many hundreds of magazine articles, Ian has four other published books to his credit, These are available as follows:

The Airgun Hunters Year, published by Merlin Unwin. ISBN 978-1-906122-28-7
www.merlinunwin.co.uk

Airgun Fieldcraft, published by Blaze Publishing. ISBN 978-0-9549597-2-2
www.blazepublishing.co.uk

The Hunters Way, available on Kindle. ASIN: B00HG09Q0M
www.amazon.co.uk/The-Hunters-Tao-Ian-Barnett-ebook/dp/B00HG09Q0M

Hobby Writing – How To Make Your Play, Pay, available on Kindle. ASIN: B00IBL5QOK
www.amazon.co.uk/Hobby-Writing-Make-Your-Play-ebook/dp/B00IBL5QOK

Printed in Great Britain
by Amazon.co.uk, Ltd.,
Marston Gate.